REFRACTIONS
WRITERS AND PLACES

REFRACTIONS
WRITERS AND PLACES

BY

Robert Packard

Carroll & Graf Publishers, Inc.
New York

Copyright © 1990 by Robert Packard
All rights reserved

First Carroll & Graf Edition 1990

Carroll & Graf Publishers, Inc
260 Fifth Avenue
New York, NY 10001

Library of Congress Cataloging-in-Publication Data

Refractions : writers and places / Robert Packard. — 1st Carroll
& Graf ed.
    p.   cm.
  ISBN 0-88184-576-0 : $17.95
  1. Travel in literature.   2. Historic sites in literature.
3. Setting (Literature)   I. Title.
PN56.T7P34   1990
809'.93355—dc20   90-31727
                                                        CIP

Manufactured in the United States of America

Refractions: Writers and Places

Introduction		3
Chapter One:	Homer and Chaucer's Troy	7
Chapter Two:	Proust's Illiers-Combray	25
Chapter Three:	Byron's Sintra	43
Chapter Four:	Dostoyevsky's Florence	61
Chapter Five:	Irving's Alhambra	77
Chapter Six:	Mark Twain's Venice	97
Chapter Seven:	Cervantes' La Mancha	115
Chapter Eight:	Thoreau's Cape Cod	133
Index		163

Acknowledgements

Many writers acknowledge their literary debts by declaring rhetorical bankruptcy. Payment to their creditors exceeds their syntactical reach. No words exist to repay those wives, husbands, and lovers who are invariably patient, inspirational, and if the writers are lucky, typists. Essential help rendered by academicians and savants (the more celebrated the better) is acknowledged. These benefactors, often trailed by pitiful "too numerous to mention" nonentities, are awarded medals engraved "Official release from error complicity" while the flip side reads "Credit for creative felicities."

I plead guilty to writing this book without assistance: romantic, editorial, or material. No one typed it for me, tendered advice, offered ideas, or served as inspiration. The reader may consider this independence a misfortune, but it does release me from the sneaking conjecture that full responsibility for what follows lies elsewhere.

I have paraphrased freely from articles of mine that appeared in quite different form in the following publications: the *New York Times*, on Dostoyevsky, Thoreau, and Irving; *Connoisseur*, on Cervantes; *Travel & Leisure*, on Byron;

1

Oceans, on Thoreau; and *The Philadelphia Inquirer* on Irving. My colleague, Dr. Harold Dorn, did suggest the title to me just a moment before I would have thought of it myself; my agent, Peter Ginsberg, did have faith in it; and finally, Kent Carroll had the wit to recognize that a book about the confluence of writers and places needed a publisher.

Introduction
Refractions: Writers and Places

I stole the term *refraction* from optics: just as a ray of light bends as it passes obliquely from one medium to another, the image of a physical place passing through the prism of the writer's imagination changes to become the literary place.

This book is about writers and places. My first concern is the writers: they illustrate the theme of creative imagination and refraction. They include three poets— one Greek and two from England: a novelist each from Spain, France, America, and Russia; and two essayists from America.

I chose the writers; they chose the places.

They journey to cities of the imagination in both classical Greece and medieval England; to a mountain aerie in Portugal; to a French provincial town; to a New England seacoast; to two great Italian cities; to a Moorish palace; and to the high tableland of central Spain.

The nine writers trace the widest refractive compass: places that take shape in their writing reflect their physical models in ways that range from almost microscopic reproduction to

3

discordant abstraction. Each writer's imaginative eye creates a distinctive image of his model.

Writers we have read and places we have visited become part of our lives, but only when we shake off the constrictions of both the academic mantle of literature and the guidebook categorization of travel does this confluence take on the role of one of life's splendid pleasures. *Refractions* deals with those pleasures. The diverse writers chosen here are so evocative that apart from any discussion of refraction their ideas and images impel one to think about them, write about them, and best of all, read them.

Scarcely more than a century ago, Heinrich Schliemann excavated the ruins of a city that bore an astonishing resemblance to the Troy of *The Iliad*. But neither Homer nor Chaucer, separated from one another by two thousand years, had a physical model for the Troys they wrote about. Their Troys are based on the refracted vision of what they had heard and read, and indeed all the Troys of literature are cities of the imagination. Homer's Troy is Greek, Chaucer's is English, neither is Trojan.

Proust's transformation of Illiers, a French provincial town of remarkable conventionality, to Combray, that dwelling place of the mind in *Remembrance of Things Past*, is a masterly example of refraction at the core of a great literary work. Illiers now calls itself Illiers-Combray, an ironic tribute—with one eye on tourism—made in the vain hope that a casual hyphen could somehow unite Combray and Illiers. Travelers looking for Combray will not find it in Illiers; Combray belongs immutably to *Remembrance*.

The town of Sintra suffers from a two-hundred-year headache brought on by trying to justify Byron's romantic extravagance when he referred to this Portuguese aerie as a "glorious Eden" in *Childe Harold*. Sintra's architecture reflects an enthusiasm for structures aspiring, often ludicrously, for ethereal stature; the thriving tourist industry promotes Byronic sites and schlock souvenirs.

When it comes to instances of a writer's imagination causing a site not only to alter but in so doing to become a multimillion-dollar travel attraction, Washington Irving's Alhambra brooks no rivals. Irving's lens showed a ruin, his glossy print a palace. The discrepancy between the Alhambra of Irving's residence and his romantic version of that perception is a lesson in the vagaries of refraction. That his fantasy should become the reality of today's Alhambra is as unlikely as it is engaging.

No better example exists of a writer's slanted vision than Dostoyevsky's insistence that Florence, where he lived for almost a year, was a hell worse than Siberia (where he lived for eight). In his letters and journals he applied his brush vigorously to a canvas purportedly evoking Florence, but every stroke etched a self-portrait.

In order to attract as many newspaper readers as possible, Mark Twain wrote about Venice as if it were an Arkansas town in flood; but Samuel Clemens, who invented him, had a different view. Here is a sterling example of a refracted image deliberately obscured by the artifice of pseudonymity.

If a literary analogy exists between what optics forbiddingly calls "birefringence"—the splitting of a light ray into two components that are polarized at right angles to each other—*Don Quixote* is that instance. Cervantes gave one La Mancha, prosaic and literal, to Sancho Panza, and another—its polarized antithesis—to Don Quixote. Anyone romantic enough to travel to La Mancha today in search of either one is in for a big surprise: both of them are still there.

Henry Thoreau was not so much concerned with the literary recreation of places as with what lay beneath their surfaces. Like Proust, he finds his meaning here. His eye for detail—unsentimentalized and highly sensitized—

allowed him to give uncommon resonance to a stretch of Cape Cod seacoast.

Writers and travel are one of life's true enrichments. I found the pleasures of exploring the literary imagination by means of refraction to be a freedom from the constraints of historical and literary categorization, the limitations of genres, and the frontiers of travel.

It's anyone's planet. Each one of us carries in his mind a view of the world based on an individual variation of the external model. But unlike most of us, writers give their worlds perceptible substance. What follows is a look at the effects of refraction when nine literary figures focus on places of concern to them. The results are surprising.

1

Homer and Chaucer's Troy

HOMER INVENTED TROY. HE TOOK WHAT HE WANTED FROM a chimerical past to create a city for his *Iliad*. Homer wrote of Troy as if it were a neighboring worldly locale of his acquaintance, even though at least five hundred years separated him from his imagined city. In the legends of this past glimmered an illustrious site besieged and destroyed by the vengeful Greeks.

Homer described Troy with such economy that he freed countless writers to reshape his city as a reflection of their own thematic concerns. Homer's city plan for Troy has few specific details. Mere generalities prevail. His Troy is windy and spacious. Priam's palace, the the dwellings of the offspring of his absurdly fecund marriage to Hecuba, appear in sparing outline. We learn something of the walls and the bastion and the gates that lead to the battlefield, where Homer's primary interest lay. But that is all.

Two thousand years after Homer, Chaucer created another Troy for *Troilus and Cressida*—this one in affectionate detail. Chaucer, separated now by almost twenty-six hundred years from the original Troy, and with no historical evidence to get in his way, writes knowingly of Troy's palaces, gardens, and bedrooms. Homer is epic, Chaucer domestic. Homer deals with the sweep of human destiny, Chaucer with the poignancy of individual fate.

Chaucer's medieval Troy is a sophisticated city with only a hint of the horrendous battles being waged outside its walls. The war serves as an opportunity for Chaucer's Trojans to display their heroism in such a way that it will enhance their amorous proclivities off the battlefield, while on it they can attack the Greeks with chivalric panache. His Trojans gather in public places for festivals, attend houseparties at country estates, go hunting during times of truce, and dine elegantly in one another's well-appointed mansions. Chaucer's Trojans dwell in medieval England.

Homer and Chaucer see Troy at the same moment during the Trojan War: like its mortal inhabitants, the city is doomed to die. Their characters share recognizable names, but they exist in philosophical worlds as distinctive as those of their creators. In both poems Troy conducts much of its daily business curiously undeterred by the nine-year siege focusing on its capitulation.

Within a year the city will be desecrated, burned, and pillaged by its maddened Greek conquerors. Historically, it will lie in ruins to be identified as Strata VIIa of the Troys that Heinrich Schliemann uncovered a century ago in his aberrant excavations. But the literary Troys far outnumber the archaeological layers of ancient cities built upon the ruins of their predecessors. From its varied literary manifestations fictional Troy keeps rising phoenixlike, in distinctive and often startling forms.

Troy, the first city to appear in Western literature, illustrates the paradox of fictional visions and the disparate sites they spawn. Troy changes and alters to accommodate every writer after Homer who chooses the city as his *mise-en-scène*. Myth links the Troy of Homer and that of Chaucer; their distinctive Troys arise from the thematic content of their individual poems. And this link and these distinctions are true of all of Troy's fictional manifestations. The walls are the single unifying structural element. When the site itself was excavated, there lay the crumbled walls.

We know nothing about Homer; his identity rests obscure. Herodotus, from a distance of some three hundred years and bolstered by no concrete evidence, surmises that Homer lived in the ninth century B.C. Scholars today contend that Homer lived not later than the eighth century. Both *The Iliad* and *The Odyssey* acquired substantially their present form when Athens' sixth-century tyrant, Pisistratus, commissioned a learned body to establish definitive texts. The present structure of the poems, with their division into books, originated with Alexandrine critics.

Ignorance makes us uneasy. Homer's empty biographical throne seems like a rebuke. The urge to place a straw man (or men) upon it proved irresistible. Seven cities vied with one another for the honor of being his birthplace. Smyrna, now Turkey's Izmir, made the loudest claims. The island of Ios maintained that he died there. The island of Chios, on the basis of the Hymn to the Delian Apollo, insisted that Homer, old and blind, dwelt on its shores.

We know as little about the Trojan War as we do about Homer. But here at least we have some archaeological evidence of cities destroyed, and some scholarly historical support to the supposition of conflicts between aggressors on the Greek peninsula and those who lived near the entrance to the Black Sea. The rest is myth. Troy's preordained fate gives the city a tragic cast: its purportedly impregnable defenses seem all too flawed. The ruse of the Trojan horse pits deception against gullibility and the former deserves to win.

Homer called Troy the favorite city of Zeus. What this unsavory god of gods favored was bound to shimmer at least briefly in the light of his mercurial patronage. Zeus wants to spare Troy destruction at the hands of the Greeks, but not at the cost of marital discord for himself. He taunts his spouse Hera with her malicious desire "to sack the lovely town of Troy." He tells her of his strong bond with Troy, a city that understood well his acquisitive arrogance: ". . . of all the cities that men live in under the sun and starry sky, the nearest to my heart was holy Ilium, with Priam and the people of Priam of the good ashen spear. Never at their banquets did my altar go without its proper share of wine and fat, the offerings that we claim as ours."

Not every culture invents a supreme diety who openly concedes that his beneficence depends upon a proper share of wine and fat. But Hera will have none of his importuning. Momentarily distracted from serving nectar in gold tankards, she reminds her husband that while she is his consort, they are children of the same father. She, too, is divine.

Hera claims Argos, Sparta, and Mycenae as the three towns (inevitably Greek) she holds dearest to her heart. She promises Zeus that if any of them become "obnoxious" to him, she will not grudge him their destruction nor make a stand on their behalf.

Apart from this chilling spectral Olympian glance, Troy appears in *The Iliad* solely from the perspective of the omniscient narrator and his characters. Troy's outstanding feature is that high wall encircling its structures and protecting it from intrusion. Built by Poseidon, the wall seems to have one principal exit, the Scaean Gate. The gate has wooden doors, held firmly in place with bars. Sentries do guard duty there.

Through this Scaean Gate the Trojans depart daily to fight the Greeks on the plains. The old men of the town line the wall to see how the war is progressing, somewhat like season-ticket holders. The women go there from time to time to see how their husbands and/or lovers are faring.

In what Homer calls "the neighborhood of this gate" stands

an observation tower. This is the prime battlefield lookout. Here we first see King Priam, sitting in conference with his counselors and the elders of the city. Too old to fight, they "sat there on the tower, like cicadas perched on a tree in the woods chirping delightfully."

This image of the inhabitants of the besieged city chirping delightfully within range of the battlefield establishes a tone for Homer's treatment of Troy that seems more Chekhovian than Homeric. The abduction of Helen by Paris is the stuff of musical comedy. The city walls become the bedroom door; Helen's husband Menelaus is on the far side loudly demanding admittance. Homer's Troy is curiously at odds with the epical nature of the poem.

On this morning the old men see the Greek and Trojan forces sitting quietly leaning on their spears. Menelaus and Paris stand facing one another on the vast plain. They have agreed to fight a duel. The winner will claim Helen as his wife. The armies have been threatening one another "with a terrible battle," but the proposed treaty following the duel will offer "a reprieve from the painful business of fighting."

Inside the palace Helen works at her weaving. "On a great purple web of double width [she depicts] some of the many battles between the horsetaming Trojans and the bronze-clad Achaens in the war that had been forced upon them for her sake." Helen's egocentricity aside, she is rarely given scholarly credit for her role as a dedicated historian. As a symbol for the manifold rationale for war—the trust betrayed, the revenge aglitter—Helen serves *The Iliad* well. As a character, she is patiently absurd. Irrational, inconsistent, and lovely beyond words, she inhabits *The Iliad* like a sexy wraith, admonishing herself as a slut, castigating her current "husband" Paris for his lack of resolve, filled "with tender longing for her former husband and her parents and the city she had left." Just beneath the conscience-stricken surface of her mind lies the reassuring awareness that her beauty and her person have the power to make cataclysmic the world of which she is a part.

Where does Helen live in Troy? She dwells with Paris in what Homer calls "a splendid house." Paris had built this dwelling himself, with the best workmen to be found in the fertile land of Troy. They built it for him, complete with sleeping quarters, hall, and courtyard, close to Priam's and Hector's houses on the Acropolis.

Not unexpectedly, the only room we see in what Homer terms "the beautiful house of Paris" is the bedroom. And even here we are confined to essentials. The room is lofty, the bed wooden and well made. When Paris is not on the battlefield, acquitting himself with dubious valor (and a great deal of assistance from the gods), and when Helen is not busy with her weaving, they lie down together on this bed. She is as irresistible as she is weak-willed, and he as lusty as he is simple-minded.

In limiting his architectural outline of Troy to a few palatial dwellings in his "spacious" city, Homer leaves most of the blueprint untouched. Empty space abounds, a gift for future writers and imaginative readers. Homer sketches a town entirely subordinate to the larger needs and themes of his masterwork. Priam's palace compound alone (an unexpected precursor of today's "townhouse" complexes) is described in some detail. And even here a bemused Homer's major concern is how a mythic Trojan king provides suitable residence for his family of fifty sons and twelve daughters.

Priam's palace is the stellar building in Troy. On the Acropolis, conceivably the highest point in the city, it is fronted with marble colonnades. The residence boasts "scented storerooms." Those fifty sons and their wives dwell behind the palace in fifty apartments of polished stone adjoining one another. A motel-like arrangement of twelve contiguous bedrooms of the same polished stone provide accommodation for his daughters. Here Priam's sons-in-law "slept with their loving wives" in these separate quarters across the courtyard.

Hector, as Priam's eldest son and Troy's heroic counterpart to the Greeks' Achilles, lives near his father's palace in a house (like his brother Paris) that Homer simply calls "well built." The same term is used to describe the wide streets of the city as Hector rushes down them in search of Andromache, his wife, who has climbed the great tower of Ilium near the Scaean Gate to see how martial matters are progressing.

In addition to the royal palace, the city must hold mansions of those of great wealth. Young Trojans on the battlefield plead for their lives, promising that from their homes filled with bronze and gold and wrought iron their fathers would gladly pay a fortune in ransom. Adrestus pleads thus to Menelaus, and another Trojan, Dolon, uses almost identical terms in supplicating Odysseus.

The opulence of Troy's populace further suggests that they may well have lived in splendid houses, if their attire is any criterion. The Trojan women wore elegant gowns; the farther their robes trailed behind them the better. In her storeroom Hecuba selected an embroidered gown, the work of Sidonian women, to offer as a sacrifice to Athena. Paris himself had picked out the robe for her when "he was on the cruise that brought him home with highborn Helen." Hecuba selected this longest and most richly decorated dress as her gift for Athena. It had lain underneath all the rest and now glittered like a star.

On the Acropolis stood the temple of Athena. When Hecuba went there to pray for the defeat of the Greeks, her pleas and offerings were to no avail. Athena shook her head; she would not be swayed by gifts of high fashion. Even with the robe laid invitingly on her knees, the goddess was implacable.

The men of Troy were not precisely drab in their attire. When Paris is not buck-naked in the bedroom, he is resplendent as the dazzling sun. Around his well-shaped legs he wears a pair of splendid greaves, fitting with silver clips for the ankles. On his breast he sports a cuirass, over his shoulder he slings a bronze sword with a silver-studded hilt. He carries a great thick shield. His headgear is a helmet with a horsehair crest. Fitted to his grip is a powerful spear.

Bronze-clad Hector has a glimmering helmet. So formidable is he in battle dress that his little boy, Astyanax, frightened by the shining helmet and the horsehair plume nodding grimly down on him, bursts into tears at the sight of his father.

Among the well-heeled Trojan warriors, Glaucus wears golden armor. After an agreeable chat with Diomede about their mutually distinguished heritage, he foolishly exchanged his resplendent apparel for the Greek's suit of bronze armor. Homer, ever alert to material values, points out that on a scale of one hundred, Glaucus ended up with a nine.

Whatever the historical period, modes of transportation reflect the economic status of those they transport. In Troy, the top echelon have chariots. King Priam's is best. The horses are fast and the chariot itself is—to use one of Homer's favorite terms—splendid. When Priam, accompanied by his charioteer, Antenor, drives through the gates in order to be present at the abortive peace treaty, he brings along a gleaming bowl and golden cups. Clearly, the Greeks have more to gain by capturing Troy than simply returning Helen to the arms of her loving Menelaus.

The walls of Troy and wooden gates are as tempting to the Greeks as they are reassuring to the Trojans. Agamemnon, the Greek commander-in-chief, issues an edict: "Bring down the walls of Ilium." Hector, his Trojan counterpart, vows that no cowardice on his part would permit the Greeks to enter the city by scaling the walls.

Midway in the narrative, Homer tells us that

Old King Priam climbed one of the bastions that Poseidon
had built and saw the gigantic Achilles driving the panic
stricken Trojans in utter impotence before him. Priam
gave a cry of alarm, and came down from the bastion to
give fresh orders to the tired watchmen posted by the
wall to look after the gates, "Hold the gates open," he
said, "till our routed forces reach the town. They have
Achilles at their heels, and I fear a massacre. Directly
they are sheltered by the walls and can breathe once
more, close the wooden doors."

Certainly the walls provided the Trojan warriors with a
domestic base. After a day of battle they came home to their
loving wives and children. The Greeks, encamped near their
ships, had no such amenities. Their quarters were makeshift.
For companionship they had concubines, the rewards of various campaigns. *Their* loving wives and children were at
home on the Greek mainland or on the Aegean and Ionian
islands. Agamemnon's loving wife, Clytemnestra, was at home
loving his cousin Agisthus.

Whether Homer intended Troy, with its household luxury
and ease, to be compared disadvantageously as a locale for
warriors with the harshness of the Greek camp is a moot
point. The reader is irresistibly drawn to the image of the
Trojans leaving by the Scaean Gate every morning like so
many commuters on their way to jobs that offered periods of
truce as vacation time.

Homer's parsimonious treatment of Troy supports the claim
that *The Iliad*, the "premier" literary work of the European
West, is in fact a late product of a refined poetic tradition.
Homer deftly keeps Troy as background for his emphasis on
the heroic figure of Achilles. The Greeks, not the Trojans,
are Homer's protagonists. Troy will be their prize of victory.
Homer's concern is the contest; let others describe the prize.

Many of his successors found Troy, as a disaster waiting to

happen, irresistible. Why restrict oneself to the ninth year when the tenth brought tragic drama in its most obvious manifestations? Euripides agonized over the plight of the Trojan women; Virgil dramatized the escape after the conflagration. The story of Troy's downfall becomes the backbone of Western culture. Homer's munificent gift is not reimbursable.

Homer's Troy is fashioned for war, Chaucer's for love.

Some two millennia after Homer, when Chaucer in the 1380s created his Troy as the setting for the love affair of Troilus and Cressida, he wrote as if it were an English urban center of the Middle Ages. And while all the Troys in literature stem from the seed planted by Homer, Chaucer's Troy chronologically follows the Italian model that Boccaccio devised for *Il Filostrato*, the direct source of *Troilus and Cressida*. Boccaccio's source in turn was Benoit de Sainte-Maure's *Le Roman de Troie*, c.1160. Benoit, for his part, had called upon the sixth-century *Ephemeris Belli Trojani* by Dictys Cretenis, and the fourth-century *De Excidio Trojae Historia* by Dares Phygius. Following Chaucer, Caxton's first English printing, *Recuyell of the Historyes of Troy* was in debt to Benoit, and Shakespeare's "false Cressid" to Caxton and to Chaucer himself.

Chaucer refuses to acknowledge any sources. He claims to be translating from a Latin text by one Lollius, about whom nothing was ever heard before or since. When Chaucer wants to avoid responsibility for the unsavory and inexplicable actions of his characters, particularly Cressida's nefarious betrayal, he claims to be at the mercy of his translation. Thus Chaucer had his little joke while deftly averting attention from his direct indebtedness to Boccaccio.

Chaucer probably knew Homer through Latin translations. Greek texts were not yet a part of English culture; the Renaissance crept slowly westward from Italy. But Chaucer had precedents in giving his Troy a British flavor. Both

Geoffrey of Monmouth, in his twelfth-century *Historia Regum Britanniae*, and Chaucer's contemporary, John Gower, in his *Vox Clamantis*, an account of the Peasants' Revolt in 1381, had referred to London as "New Troy." Likening London to Troy had political overtones: Troy's downfall was attributed by some to moral decay in both the royal family and the nobility. Chaucer's Cressida betrayed her lover for one of the enemy; her father, Calchus, betrayed Troy itself; Helen's abduction by Paris, the brother of Troilus, instigated the fatal Trojan war. Chaucer even gives his Troy a Parliament, the most unlikely establishment ever bestowed upon the city by one of its re-creators.

Chaucer, as urbane a literary practitioner as ever wrote a line of English poetry, had his Trojan lovers follow fashions of dalliance current in the fourteenth-century literary Christendom; he pictured his Greek and Trojan warriors as chivalric knights in medieval armor, his maidens as gentle hearts on whom troths could be plighted. The formal religion throughout the poem is pagan (Greek gods and goddesses incongruously bearing Roman names in this cultural bouillabaise) and the lovers first see one another in the courtship tradition of Dante and Petrarch at the "temple" on the feast of the Palladian; yet the characters speak of God as if they were Christians with souls to save and salvation to swear by.

Thus Chaucer freed himself from the bindings of Christian ethics in matters of sex: his lovers could have their *amor* and consummate it, too. The one code to observe was that of courtly love, a medieval literary concept so far removed from the mores of the ancient Greeks and Trojans as to give it at once an absurd poignancy. Playing off one historical period against the other, taking what served his purpose, Chaucer liberates his characters from the guilt of libidinous gratification. The hidden courtly-love trap insists that the lady should never be sullied by gossip or comment. To observe this stricture, the lovers must separate, and the stage is set for deception.

Chaucer, brilliantly fusing these distinctive historical and cultural periods, knew precisely what he was doing. The result is that sparks fly from wheels set in motion to create friction, leaving behind the well-oiled predictability of the myth of the Trojan War to serve as a convenient backdrop.

Chaucer's view of Troy as a city whose impregnable walls offer protection against military might—but not against cunning—is one held by all writers who employ the myth of the Trojan War. Troy without walls is unthinkable. Ontogeny recapitulates phylogeny. Excavations begun in the late nineteenth century at Hassarlik, some four miles from the Turkish coastline, and continued since then, confirm that all the ancient cities on the Trojan mound (well before and after Homer's time) were walled. Cunning is eternal.

Chaucer's walls, like Homer's, are interrupted by a main gate giving access to the battlefield plains beyond and to the seacoast of the Greek encampment. When Cressida leaves Troy to join her father, Calchas, in the Greek camp, ostensibly for ten days, Troilus goes to the gate to see her depart. With hawk in hand, Troilus "with a splendid rout of knights" rides forth to keep her company until they passed a distant valley and were obliged to return. His love for her is locked in the courtly-love code of secrecy. Antenor (Priam's charioteer in *The Iliad*), for whom Cressida was being exchanged, appears en route to his beloved walled city, and Troilus, his eyes filled with tears for the departing Cressida, embraces and welcomes him.

The walls of Troy once again serve to highlight drama.

As the days draw to a close, Troilus returns to the gate to recapture somehow his last glimpse of Cressida. He walks up and down atop the walls, gazing toward the Greek "host" in the distance. For her part, Cressida peers ruefully back at the tall towers and "halls" of Troy, remembering the joy that had been hers within Troy's walls. Chaucer's Troy, unlike Homer's, is within distant sight of the tents of the Greek encampment.

At last comes the promised day for Cressida's return. Troilus and Pandar "ply" the walls of the town. Nothing. Returning later, Troilus decides to go to the gate itself to make sure that the "uncunning" porters don't close it. "Cometh eve," Troilus looks forth "by hegge, by tree, by greve / And fer his heed over the wal he leyde" even imagining that a distant "farecart" might be Cressida on horseback.

Darkness falls. The Warden of the Gates begins to call those outside the walls, telling them either to drive in their cattle or be denied entrance. Then Troilus, "with many a tear" rides homeward. Like all of us since time immemorial whose lovers have failed to keep an appointment, Troilus rationalizes that he misunderstood the time and the day. Next morning he returns to the gate, paces up and down, looks east and west: "Upon the walles made he many a wente / But al for nought." At last, Troilus knows that Cressida will not keep her promise. He can think of no other remedy but to prepare himself to die.

Chaucer's Troy, like Homer's, is filled with palatial dwellings. But Chaucer does not limit himself to the residence of the royal family. Homes in this medieval city are often called palaces, in the sense that Italian Renaissance mansions are termed *palazzi*. Cressida's house is no exception. After Calchus defects to the Greeks, she becomes mistress of the palace "with such in her employ as it concerned her honor to uphold." When she goes to a dinner party at Pandar's house she is accompanied by "certain of her own men [servants], her niece Antigone, and other of her women nine or ten."

Cressida's house faces the street that runs from the Dardanus (Scaean) Gate to the royal palace. The dwelling contains a "paved parlor" with benches; windows with lattice protection open onto the street. The house has an interior medieval walled garden. The garden has interweaving sanded paths, and is "shadowed well with blossomy green boughs, newly benched." Cressida's bedroom is on the second floor. From her window she listens to the song of the nightingale coming from a "cedar green under the chamber-wall." Her house has a dining hall in which there are window seats. Here Pandar persuades her to write to Troilus, a delicate step for her to take in the labyrinthian course of courtly love.

"Depardieux," says Cressida, a Trojan lady using a French term bought to medieval England by way of the Norman Conquest, "God grant that all will be well."

The royal palace in which Troilus lives is conceivably just one of the fifty apartments created by Homer for Priam and his progeny. But we see only Troilus's bedroom, in which he passed countless hours of lovelorn torment, suffering from a particularly acute case of "lover's complaint," known to every chivalric knight who ever enmeshed himself in the thorny patches of courtly love. We see somewhat more of the residence of his brother, Deiphebus, who agrees to give a king of cocktail-reception-dinner party ostensibly to discuss a lawsuit of Cressida's but actually a trumped-up complicated device of Pandar's to arrange the first actual meeting of Troilus and Cressida following their correspondence.

The guest list includes a number of Troy's rich and famous, not least the lady of the decade, the beauteous Helen. Cressida is accompanied by her niece, Antigone. When dinner is served, Deiphebus "did them great honor and fed them well with all that they might like." (Chaucer is wary of the specifics of Trojan cuisine.) But Troilus is absent. He is upstairs in a bed enclosed by medieval curtains, ill with some fake fever for which everyone at the party advances a real remedy.

After discussing Cressida's simulated legal problem, Helen suggests that it would be a good idea if Cressida were to visit Troilus briefly to acquaint him with the matter and solicit his aid. "And by your leave," says Helen, "I'll just pop in and see if he's asleep." Awake he was, and Helen "in her goodly soft way gave him greeting and began to play womanly and lay her arm right over his shoulder and with all her wit attempted to comfort and amuse him." Helen's "wit" is eternal: Chaucer's Troy is different from Homer's, but the passing of two thousand years has not altered Helen.

Pandar's house serves as the scene of the lovers' assignation. Pandar, choosing the rain-swept weather deviously, invites Cressida to evening supper with him; he hides Troilus in a nearby closet of his bedroom. Troilus has been there since midnight of the previous evening; such was the endurance of courtly lovers in the interests of secrecy. No stain must fall on Cressida's reputation. She confesses later that she was not entirely surprised by the ruse, and indeed she would otherwise have been a blockhead.

Cressida arrives with her entourage of at least twelve persons. Pandar receives them and leads them one by one into supper where no "dainties" of any kind are lacking. After supper comes entertainment. He sings. She plays. But when it is time to leave, "all was in a flood," and Pandar persuades her to spend the night in his home.

Pandar has anticipated all the sleeping arrangements. The ladies-in-waiting are to sleep in the "middle chamber," and Cressida in his "little closet yonder" beyond whose door should there be a disturbance will be the ladies to protect her. In due course, he tells her that in his bedroom awaits Troilus, who has arrived there "through a gutter, by a private way . . . unknown to anyone."

In one of the great comic scenes of English literature, Troilus, finally brought to Cressida's bedside, promptly faints, and this "mouse's heart"—as Pandar derisively calls him— must be stripped of his clothes and placed beside her in the bed. Pandar can do no more. He takes a light, retreats to the fireplace, and arranges his countenance as if he were "looking upon an old romance."

Comes the Trojan dawn, "the cruel day, denouncer of the joy that night and lover have stolen." Troilus must leave for his "royal palace" where "softly in his bed he began to slink."

Chaucer's chivalric knights set out every morning for the battlefield, creating a kind of martial rush hour as their steeds crowded the streets. They returned—if they were lucky—every evening to the plaudits of the citizenry leaning from their balconies. In times of truce, the activities in Chaucer's Troy constituted a nice mingling of English domestic and Trojan exotic. Troilus rides out hawking, or else "he hunts the boar, the bear, or the lion." Troilus makes a point of leaving "small beasts" untouched and unpursued. When he returns to town, from some never specified countryside, Cressida is often waiting at her window to salute him (secretly, of course) "as fresh as a falcon coming out of the cage."

Later in the poem, at a time when Pandar is trying to distract Troilus from his torment over the absence of Cressida, the two men spend a week as houseguests of Sarpedoun during a time of truce. This Sarpedoun, "an honorable man all of his life," maintained a mansion apparently devoted exclusively to lavish entertainment. Sarpendoun's residence seems to be in the English countryside directly beyond the walls of Troy. Daily his table was laid with costly "dainties," and he entertained with such liberality that everyone said that heretofore no feast had known the equal. Nor was this all. No instrument in the musical world was lacking at the feasts, "no company so fair as the ladies dancing there."

Troilus wants to leave. For four days he can think of nothing but Cressida. He returns to town. Better to be where she no longer is than where she has never been. Chaucer takes us on a sentimental tour of Troy as Troilus seeks out sites that seem haunted by her absence. When Troilus looks at the palace of Cressida he sees not only a building in which his love no longer dwells but one that is literally boarded up, as if to repudiate its function as a place for human occupation. He finds the doors sparred across, the windows barred. This desolate palace, the architectual metaphor of his emotional state, this "crown of houses, now forsaken" seems to Troilus like a shrine whose saint has departed. The doors are cold, even as the heart of Troilus is "frosted over."

He passes the temple where he had first seen her, standing there so modestly close by the door; he rides by a neighboring house in which he remembers first having heard her sing; and at a secluded spot "yonder" he recalls her laughter and above all her words of love.

At the gates of Troy he looks out to the hill where on that fateful morning of her departure he had been compelled to turn back. Troy has become a city of memory, painful to live in, redolent of that which it no longer contains. What was once a vibrant metropolis, alive with amorous intrigue and excitement, hospitable and open to the consummation of love's desire, is now closed and empty.

"Go, little book," writes Chaucer at the conclusion of *Troilus and Cressida*, "go my little tragedy." He has no wish to set up his poem in comparison with the work of the masters, and he "kisses the gracious footsteps" of Homer, Virgil, Ovid, and Statius. His own Troy is as memorable as any ever created: the fusion of pagan and Christian elements together with the melding of classical values and the code of medieval courtly love give his Troy a vibrant, shimmering quality.

Unlike the seven writers in subsequent chapters of this book, whose refractive perspectives of places stem from actual models, the Troys of Homer and Chaucer are cities of the imagination, disparate views of what proved upon archaeological excavation to be the ruins of a Troy destroyed at the time of the presumptive Trojan War. As Strata VIIa, their Troy had been chillingly relegated to a stratification statistic among the many Troys piled atop one another like layers of an elaborate cake. Those literal Troys, formidable and concrete, rising proudly on that high mound near the mouth of the Black Sea, have crumbled; the fictional Troys, fragile and abstract, rising from the imagination of their creators, have survived.

2

Proust's Illiers-Combray

PROUST'S NARRATOR IN *REMEMBRANCE OF THINGS PAST* speaks of a nostalgic longing for impossible journeys through the realms of time. Proust's childhood and youthful sojourns at Illiers, a town in northwest central France, becomes his narrator's impressionistic recollections of Combray. Proust disguises Illiers for practical reasons: he wishes to free himself from the factual constraints of autobiographical recollection; and he needs to protect the sanctity of those recollections from trespassers.

Combray, then, emerges as an imaginary town rooted in the constraining reality of Illiers. Today we have both at our disposal. The fictional town does not change. The actual one has altered: time, and the fame that attended Proust's novel have made Illiers aware of itself as a setting of a literary masterpiece. We visit Illiers today but we are seeking Combray.

Proust's vast novel in the 1981 Moncrieff–Kilmartin translation is 3,294 pages long. A good part of the first of three volumes is given over to Combray, but the entire work is embued with the essence of this location. So vividly and so sensitively are Combray and its surroundings impressed upon the narrator's memory that it becomes the mainspring of the novel's sensibility.

"The capital of Proust's universe, the sun about which his worlds revolve, is the village of Combray," wrote Lewis Galantiere in 1928. Out of Combray comes the germ of all the successful characters of the novel, foremost among them the narrator. Proust's masterly creation of this narrator, hesitantly named Marcel, only understood as the embodiment of Proust's spirit, comes to us first as a youth who lives in Paris but whose sensibility is rooted in Combray.

From Combray, Proust's refracted Illiers, come the portraits of his family and of the inimitable Françoise, a servant who causes the reader to smile with anticipatory pleasure whenever her name appears on a page. From Combray come Swann, the Guermantes, Legrandin, Vinteuil, and Bloch, and with them the church of Saint-Hilaire and its shifting steeples, the hawthorn blossoms, and the water lilies. Combray is the source, the light, the means by which the novel takes shape and develops into a creation that sometimes disguises its apparent distance from later thematic concerns but which never separates itself from the seed of memory.

Almost certainly the most immediate identification with *Remembrance of Things Past* by readers and even nonreaders is the celebrated incident of the morsel of "petit madeleine" cake dipped in a spoonful of tea. Until that transcendent moment, the narrator's conscious memory of Combray had centered on a single place and instant, isolated from all their possible surroundings, detached and solitary against a shadowy background. It was "as though all Combray had consisted of but two floors joined by a slender staircase, and as though there had been no time but seven o'clock at night." By an exercise of the will, he could have recalled other scenes and other hours. But that kind of intellectual memory, he maintains, would bring with it pictures that show a past that preserves nothing of the past itself.

Such a Combray was dead, very possibly permanently. It is a labor in vain to attempt to recapture our past, Proust writes. All the efforts of our intellect must prove futile. The past is hidden somewhere outside the realm, beyond the reach of intellect. In the case of Combray it lay hidden in the sensation that the material object of the madeleine brought to the narrator. Between his childhood years in Combray and that revelation many years had elapsed during which nothing of Combray remained but his bedroom and the time of retiring.

The sensation brought about by the tasting of the tea-soaked morsel did not bring immediate recognition of its original source. An intense struggle ensued between stimulus and revelation. Proust's narrator cannot determine the source of that exquisite pleasure that invades his senses. It was individual, detached, with no suggestion of its origin. While instigating the taste and aroma, it infinitely transcends these savors and could not be of the same nature as theirs.

He drinks a second mouthful, and another, but the progression lessens rather than increases the sensation brought on by the first. He must do more than seek; he must create. Something which does not exist must be given reality and substance. The unremembered state, bringing with it a sense of happiness, was a real state in whose presence other states of consciousness melted and vanished.

Undoubtedly what he is seeking, what is "palpitating in the depth," of his being must be the image, the visual memory that, linked to the taste, tries to follow it into his conscious mind. Ten times over he attempts the discovery, stopping his ears and inhibiting all attention to the sounds that come from the next room. He resists the temptation to give in to the natural laziness that deters one from every difficult enterprise and to leave the thing alone, drink his tea, and think merely of the present, with its own complement of worries and hopes.

Suddenly the memory returns. The taste was that of the little crumb of madeleine which on Sunday mornings at Combray his Aunt Léonie used to give him from her own cup of real or lime-flower tea. Combray is his reward:

> The street rose up like the scenery of a theatre . . . [and] in that moment all the flowers in our garden and in M. Swann's park, and the water-lilies on the Vivonne and the good folk of the village and their dwellings and the parish church and the whole of Combray and of its surroundings, taking their proper shapes and growing solid, sprang into being, town and gardens alike, from my cup of tea.

Two floors joined by a slender staircase at seven o'clock in the evening become a house, a garden, beyond them a town, and farther on to the transcendent countryside. Seven o'clock becomes morning and night and all weathers and happenings.

Proust's vast novel was originally published in eight parts, the first of which in its English translation, *Swann's Way (Du côté de chez Swann)* contains the two-hundred-page section subtitled "Combray." Volume I of the three-volume 1981 Scott-Moncrieff–Kilmartin English translation incorporated as well the second of the eight parts, *Within a Budding Grove*. The novel begins with a section titled "Overture" and it is here that we encounter the luminous moment that brings with it the remembrance of things past. Combray can now be revealed in all its textured richness.

The reader is drawn into the world of Combray with such conviction that it is difficult to recall that Combray is not a real town of autobiographical reminiscence. Proust encour-

ages this deception, falling back on the time-honored fictional device of space-lines to disguise true identity. A
demimondaine asks the narrator's uncle: "Tell me, is your
niece Mme.————" Depriving the narrator's mother of a
surname in the light of the revelation that the narrator is
named "Marcel" furthers the reader's suspicion that author
and narrator are one.

Illiers becomes Combray in the novel because it denotes the
sum of Proust's imaginative evocation of Illiers and thus
ceases to be that actual town. To call it Illiers would be false;
there are as many Illiers as there are persons whose consciousness the town has penetrated. There is only one
Combray. But that Combray is bifurcated by the passage of
time that separates Marcel's physical presence there and his
recollection of that presence. The Combray of Marcel's narrative merges childhood observations and adult introspection:
Combray is neither the Illiers that Marcel knew as a child
nor the altered one that existed concurrent with the transcendent moment of recall.

Dominating Combray is the Church of Saint-Hilaire, and
above all its steeple. As if on a pilgrimage, Marcel and his
family approached the town every year in Holy Week. The
steeple was the first sign of Combray to be seen from the
plain across which the family traveled by train. Catching
sight of it, the narrator's father would say: "Come, get
your wraps together, we are there." It was the steeple of
Saint-Hilaire that shaped and crowned and consecrated
every activity, every hour of the day, every view of the
town.

The narrator's grandmother finds in the steeple what she
prizes more than anything else, a natural air and an air of
distinction. Ignorant of architecture, she is quoted as saying:
"My dears, laugh at me if you like; it is not conventionally
beautiful, but there is something in its quaint old face that

pleases me. If it could play the piano, I'm sure it wouldn't sound tinny."

From a distance, Marcel sees "a fragment of Combray's medieval ramparts enclosed, here and there, in an outline as scrupulously circular as that of a little town in a primitive painting." And Marcel encloses the town in his circle of memory. The center of his circle is not the church of Saint-Hilaire, but the house of Aunt Léonie.

Combray's size is ideal for Proust's needs. It is large enough to be an active town, but small enough so that everyone recognizes (as distinct from knows) everyone else. Aunt Léonie, whose life since the death of her husband has been a succession of increasingly limited circumferences—first the town of Combray itself, then her house, then her bedroom, and finally her bed—observed the life of Combray from this citadel. Even the appearance of a strange dog was unsettling. At Combray a person whom one "didn't know at all" was as incredible a being as any mythological diety.

Lying in bed in the early morning, listening to sounds drift upward from the dining room where M. Swann was a guest, anxiously awaiting the arrival of his mother to kiss him goodnight, Marcel confined his Combray to the space extending from his bedroom to the periphery of his grandparent's house. At other times, the town itself counted curiously less than the country walks taken by the family. The world of Combray included two countryside walks known to Marcel as the Méséglise Way and the Guermantes Way. The first, anticipating the next sequence of the novel, was also called Swann's Way because it passed along the boundary of Swann's estate. The two ways were so distinctive that the narrator sees, far more clearly than the mere distance in miles and yards and inches separating one from the other, "the distance that there was between the parts of my brain in which I used to think of them, one of those distances of the mind which time serves only to lengthen, which separate things, irremediably from one another, keeping them for ever upon different planes."

This distance was rendered still more absolute because so diametrically opposed were the two "ways' that the family left the house by a different door, according to the way they had chosen. To set out on the Méséglise Way one left by the front door of Marcel's great-aunt's house, which opened on the Rue du Saint-Esprit. It was almost as if they were going nowhere in particular. To take the Guermantes Way, however, one left by the little gate, through the kitchen garden.

The Méséglise Way and the Guermantes Way remained linked for Marcel with that life which was the most episodic, the most full of vicissitudes: the life of the mind. The Méséglise Way with its lilacs, its hawthorns, its cornflowers, its poppies, and its apple trees; the Guermantes Way with its river full of tadpoles, its water lilies, and its buttercups, offered him for all time the image of the landscape in which he should like to live.

Perhaps, he muses, by virtue of having permanently and indissolubly united so many different impressions in his mind, simply because they made him experience them at the same time, the Méséglise and the Guermantes Ways left him exposed to much disillusionment and even to many mistakes.

The reader comes to understand that these two "Ways" are as much a part of Combray as the house of Aunt Léonie and the steeple of Saint-Hilaire. They are the limbs and extensions of Combray, an integral part of the body they grace. The adjacent countryside provides an essential background within the larger frame that constitutes Marcel's Combray. On the Méséglise walk, once Combray had been left behind, the fields unfolded unendingly, perpetually crossed, as Proust says, by invisible streams of traffic, by the wind, the tutelary genius of Combray. More than any other gift of nature on this walk, the hawthorn blossoms captured the sensibilities of the narrator. He lingers before them, losing himself in the discovery of their invisible and unchanging odor, absorbing the rhythm that disposed their flowers here and there. They offered him an indefinite continuation of the charm of youth and music, in an inexhaustible profusion, without letting him delve into this charm any more deeply.

The hawthorns are no exception to Marcel's desire to penetrate the surface enthrallment and discover the secret that lay behind it. In vain he shaped his fingers into a frame so as to have nothing but the hawthorns before his eyes; the sentiment they aroused remained obscure and vague, struggling and failing to free itself, to float across and become one with the flowers. His self-made frame reveals to him that "high up on the branches . . . a thousand buds were swelling and opening, paler in color, but each disclosing as it burst, as at the bottom of a cup of pink marble, its blood-red stain, and suggesting even more strongly than the full-blown flowers the special, irresistible quality of the hawthorn tree which, whenever it budded, whenever it was about to bloom could bud and blossom in pink flowers alone."

Along the white fence of Swann's park came first the intoxicating scent of his lilac trees and then the sight of the "plumes of white or purple blossom, which glowed, even in the shade, with the sunlight in which they had been bathed." The apple trees cast circular shadows on the sunlit ground above which the blossoms were broad petals of white satin. His enthusiasm for nature as it revealed itself splendidly in the sunshine following a storm at the edge of Montjovain Pond makes him endeavor to see more clearly the sources of his enjoyment. He learned then, as a peasant passed indifferent to him and his enthusiasms, that "identical emotions do not spring up in the hearts of all men simultaneously, by a pre-established order." Turning with affection to someone one loves, one finds that person wishing to be left undisturbed.

Because the Méséglise Way was shorter and more accessible, the family often set out on walks in uncertain weather and thus had to take refuge from the rain under trees and in gardener's huts. And this walk caused Marcel to think of Swann and his mysterious, unseen wife not accepted in bourgeois society, and his daughter whom he once saw as "a little girl, with fair, reddish hair, [with a] trowel in her hand, looking at us raising towards us a face powdered with pinkish freckles. Her black eyes gleamed." As elsewhere in the novel's section on Combray, the scene serves as a nucleus for what will be revealed later on.

When they took the Guermantes Way the family first of all made sure of fine weather. They set off, immediately after luncheon, through the little garden gate which dropped them into the Rue des Perchamps, narrow and bent at a sharp angle, dotted with grass plots over which two or three wasps would spend the day botanizing. Marcel details precisely the streets through which they would pass along by the old hostelry with its great courtyard until they arrived at the Mall, among whose treetops could be distinguished the steeple of Saint-Hilaire.

The great charm of the Guermantes Way was that they followed the course of the Vivonne river almost all the time. Across the Pont-Vieux they walked alongside a towpath overhung in summer by the bluish foliage of a hazel tree. A fisherman in a straw hat seemed to be rooted there. Then they passed fields of yellow buttercups and boys lowering glass jars into the Vivonne to catch minnows; soon the Vivonne became choked with water plants until in little ponds it was aflower with water lilies, pink, white, and here and there, on the surface, floated blushing like a strawberry, the scarlet heart of a lily set in a ring of white pearls.

Then the Vivonne once more began to flow swiftly. They would sit among the irises at the water's edge, Marcel would imagine a friendship with Mme. de Guermantes, see himself fishing for trout, drifting by himself in a boat on the Vivonne, and ask nothing more from life.

And so it was, Proust writes, that Marcel learned from the Guermantes Way to distinguish between those states which reigned alternately in his mind, during certain periods, going so far as to divide every day between them, each one returning to dispossess the other with the regularity of a fever and ague; contiguous and yet so foreign to one another, so devoid of means of communication, that he could no longer understand, or even picture himself, in one state what he had desired or dreaded or even done in the other.

It was preeminently as the deepest layer of his mental soil, as firm sites on which he could still build, that Marcel regarded the Méséglise and Guermantes Ways.

Combray appeared to Marcel, after a struggle of concentration, as the essence that emerged from the material reality of the madeleine and the lime-flower tea. And in Combray we find the theme of the entire novel. To discover what lies beneath the surface is to discover the meaning. On the Méséglise or Guermantes Way

> a roof, a gleam of sunlight reflected from a stone, the smell of a road would make me stop still, to enjoy the special pleasure that each of them gave me, and also because they appeared to be concealing, beneath what my eyes would see, something which they invited me to approach and seize from them, but which, despite all my efforts, I never managed to discover.

They seemed to be ready to open, to yield up to him the secret treasure of which they were themselves no more than the outer coverings.

These material objects, devoid of any intellectual value, and suggesting no abstract truth, gave him an unreasoning pleasure, but the effort demanded by striving for a perception of what lay hidden beneath them caused him to seek an excuse that would allow him to relax so strenuous a task and spare himself the fatigue that it involved.

Combray is the imaginary town that Proust created out of his memory of Illiers as a catalyst for the sensibilities of his protagonist. Thus Combray need not change. Rooted in memory, it can defy the vicissitudes of time. But Proust is too masterly a novelist to allow his narrator the inhuman luxury of permanence untinged by change. He concedes that one might search in vain for the Rue de Perchamps, for example, for today the public school rises upon its site. But like architects who fancy they can detect beneath a Renaissance rood-loft and an eighteenth-century altar, traces of a Norman choir, so Marcel leaves not a stone of the modern edifice standing. He pierces through the public school and restores the Rue des Perchamps.

"And for such reconstruction, memory furnished me with more detailed guidance than is generally at the disposal of restorers."

Combray, then, is Proust's refraction of Illiers, a provincial French town located in the fertile limestone tableland of Beauce. Sixty-five miles southwest of Paris, and fifteen miles south of Chartes, Illiers today has a population that hovers around three thousand.

While the Troys of Homer and Chaucer rise from legend and myth, Proust invented Combray from the intricately woven Illiers-fabric of childhood recollection and imagination. Proust's Combray bears some affinity to Byron's Sintra in that both writers, in bringing celebrity to these sites, persuaded the towns to capitalize on the image of the literary model. In each instance, life loses out to art in a mismatched competition.

In the wake of attention that followed the publication of *Remembrance of Things Past*, Illiers officially changed its name to Illiers-Combray, erecting signs to advise travelers that they were entering the town celebrated in Proust's masterpiece. But Illiers is decidedly less engaging than Combray. One sees Combray through the eyes of the most exquisite sensibility and one sees Illiers from one's own limited perspective. That perspective is limited not only because one lacks Proust's talent but because one comes to Illiers with residual memories not of the town but of the novel. What one brings to Illiers is the memory of Proust's Combray, precisely the reverse of Proust's method.

Proust's grandfather, Louis Proust, and his bride, Virginie Torcheux, kept a shop directly opposite the town church. He made wax candles for the parishioners and stocked his shop with spices, thread, sugar, and wooden shoes. They had two children. The elder, Elisabeth, became Proust's great-aunt Léonie in the novel, and the younger, Adrien, was Proust's father. The first of the family to leave Illiers, Adrien became a distinguished doctor, traveling to Persia for the French government and receiving the Légion d'honneur red ribbon from the Empress Eugénie. He married Jeanne Weil in 1870. Marcel was the first of their two sons; the second, Robert, appears nowhere in *Remembrance*.

The Proust family visited Illiers every Easter, arriving by train from their home in Paris by way of Chartres. On these visits the family stayed with Elisabeth. She had lived all her life in the village and like her fictional counterpart had reduced, in successive stages, the scope of her surroundings until she ended up permanently in her bed.

Elisabeth's husband, whom we meet in the novel only where Marcel overhears Aunt Léonie talking to herself following an ambiguous dream, was Jules Amiot, a merchant who kept a draper's shop in the marketplace of Illiers. He had spent some time in Algeria. Jules Amiot's shop was in the shadow of the steeple of Saint-Hilaire, in actuality Saint

Jacques, built in the eleventh century, renovated in the fifteenth and restored in the eighteenth to give it more of the air of the eleventh. Its name may stem from the fact that medieval pilgrims stopped there as they set out en route to Spain's Saint James of Compostella.

Very little is left of the original Romanesque church, and even some of the windows whose refracted light Proust describes in the novel were shattered in a bombing in 1940, well after his time. The side chapel whose altar in the springtime was adorned with Marcel's evocative hawthorns is the site of his first glimpse of Mme. de Guermantes.

The Rue du Saint-Esprit, onto which the family emerged from the front door of Aunt Léonie's house, is now officially named the Rue Docteur Proust. Today the house is kept open as a museum. It was given to the town to be used as such by Germaine Amiot, stepdaughter of Elisabeth Amiot, whom a plaque identifies as "Aunt Léonie." The museum is maintained by Les Amis de Marcel Proust and Les Amis de Combray, who have administered it since 1976. With the modest cost of admission comes a tour by a guide who speaks in a rapid Proustian manner and who appears to be living in Combray, not Illiers. The house itself is solidly bourgeois. If nothing else it gives one a sense of Proust's middle-class background and an insight into the novel's infatuation with the lives and mansions of the aristocracy.

The house is jam-packed with Victorian furniture of no particular distinction. In the library are Jules Amiot's Algerian mementos, not referred to in the novel. But in Aunt Léonie's room, the novel comes vividly, even poignantly, to life. Here is the famous bedside table that served double duty as a shrine and an apothecary. Here is the window from which Aunt Léonie watched the comings and goings of the people and the canines of Combray.

Almost inevitably on "Aunt Léonie's" bedside table are a teacup, a teapot, a handful of dried linden flowers, and a madeleine. One assumes that Les Amis de Marcel Proust replace it daily, an act of devotion worthy of the statue of the Madonna, also on the crowded bedside table.

On the ground floor of the house is the tile-floored kitchen. This was the province ruled by Françoise, in actuality Elisabeth Amiot's cook, Ernestine. The guide refers to the culinary delights created here as "la cuisine de Françoise." One room on this floor has been given over to a formidable collection of memorabilia. This includes not only family photographs, but period photographs of the town. Books, posters, and maps are for sale in this room, the proceeds going to the upkeep of the museum. There is a large map of Proustian places within the town that shows, as well, the surrounding countryside of the Méséglise Way (in actuality the Méséglise Way) and Tansonville, the estate of the fictional Charles Swann.

The narrator's own bedroom, which takes a central role as the catalyst of reflection in the early part of the novel, has a white canopied bed, a tapestried prie-dieu, and, beneath a bell jar, a clock so heavy that it requires a clockmaker to attend to its periodic windings. On the bedside table is a copy of George Sand's *François le Champi*, and on a side table is—one is almost tempted to say "the"—magic lantern.

The house in Illiers seems somewhat smaller than the one evoked in the novel, possibly because Proust tenanted the Combray replica with his maternal grandparents as well, neither of whom probably ever visited Illiers. The scenes of his grandmother seeking out the rain to walk in the garden come from his recollections of Auteuil, not Combray. The remark attributed to her about the church steeple, which contributes to the sense of a delightfully eccentric woman, comes from the world of metaphor.

The streets of Combray bore the solemn names of saints. With that same solemnity that caused Illiers to merge with Combray in holy hyphenation, the town changed some street names to reflect its literary heritage. Many alterations are too subtle to be caught in photographs, but on an empirical level the shops that once abutted the church are gone, and as Proust noted, the public school stands on what was once the appropriately named Rue de Perchamps. Illiers-Combray illustrates how literary imagination can alter both the face and the tone of the model.

Jules Amiot's pleasure garden on the banks of the Loire (the novel's Vivonne) is a case in point. France's Ministry of Education declared the garden a national literary site in 1946, and with the kind of unintentional irony that attends many French observations, placed several signs en route to the garden warning that the solidarity of the bridges could not be guaranteed. In this instance the irony is even Proustian.

This garden, the Pre Catalan, is across the river from Jules Amiot's vegetable garden. The Pre Catalan in the novel served as the model of both the garden of Aunt Léonie's house and the garden of Swann's Tansonville. Filled with linden and chestnut trees, its somewhat weedy outlines following a meandering tributary of the Loire, the garden has a number of dovecotes erected by Jules Amiot in an Arabic design that reminds one of his time spent in Algeria.

Today the Pre Catalan is a public park, once more administered by Les Amis de Marcel Proust. Much frequented by the citizens of Illiers, it may well have, at any given moment (as Sarah Ferrell pointed out in an 1980 *New York Times* article) a number of visitors whose grandparents or great-grandparents knew the Proust family well. From here of course one can see the omnipresent steeple of Saint Jacques, and from here, in the right season, the extravagant abundance of white and pink hawthorn blossoms.

Friday was market day in Proust's Combray and so it is today in Illiers. Everyone in Illiers (its growth caught between that of a large village and a very small town) attends the market as a purchaser or a vendor. Here are vegetables and articles of clothing, hardware and household items, flowers and bathroom fixtures. The market is a meeting place, open, somewhat raucous, a mixture of banter and venality.

George D. Painter in his landmark *Proust: The Early Years* remarked:

> It is at first sight surprising that the real landscape of Illiers should resemble so closely the created, mythical and universal landscape of Combray; and certainly in no other section of *A la Recherche du Temps Perdu* did the literal truth need so little alteration in order to make it coincide with the ideal truth.

He goes on to say that it was necessary for Proust that his Combray should be the whole novel in miniature, and contain the germ of all its themes and events.

Illiers, passing as it were obliquely through the prism of Proust's imagination, becomes that fictional Combray. Illiers may have changed its name to Illiers-Combray, but it is not Combray. It has dealt with its recognition as a Proustian site in a typically French way—one eye on culture and the other on profit. The house, now a museum, and the garden, now a public park, reflect the former. Of the latter is the madeleine skirmish among the bakers of Illiers. What visitor on home ground as it were would not want to taste one of Aunt Léonie's madeleines? Surely there is a precise location where Françoise purchased these delicacies.

Opposite the church a corner shop near the intersection of the Rues Docteur Proust (there are, incredibly, two of them, the second being the renamed Rue Cheval Blanc, on which Proust's grandfather was born) is a *pâtisserie* where a sign in the window maintains that within the shop one can find the true madeleines of Marcel Proust. But other shops ignore this claim to authenticity and purvey what has come to be known throughout the town as the Proustian madeleine.

For the visitor, a first taste of the madeleine fails inevitably to evoke a world resonant with reverberative memory—it brings instead the taste of a pleasant and in every way unremarkable plain sponge cake. In the distinction between Proust's madeleine and ours lies our engagement with the novel.

3

Byron's Sintra

L ORD BYRON DID NOT INVENT SINTRA. BUT FOLLOWING HIS
brief visit in 1809, this Portuguese hill town was never
the same. Some seventeen miles north of Lisbon, Sintra
has spent almost two hundred years striving to merit Byron's
extravagant encomium proclaiming it a "glorious Eden."
Childe Harold's Pilgrimage brought Byron international fame;
to Sintra it brought an infatuated awareness of itself as the
cynosure of romantic locales.

While Proust's invention of Combray persuaded his model,
Illiers, to draw public attention to its literary affiliation,
Byron's influence on Sintra was both more subtle and more
pervasive. Proust devotes two hundred pages of *Remembrance
of Things Past* to Combray; Byron, a half dozen seven-line
stanzas to Sintra. Yet the success of Byron's *Childe Harold's
Pilgrimage* and the subsequent fame of its author left Sintra
determined to fashion itself as a town worthy of its poetic
image. Villas and even castles began to rise on the moun-
tainsides in a Disney-like conception of Romantic structures.
Besotted burghers carved Byron's image in marble, in ivory,
in wood. Today's town plaza has as many souvenirs of Byron

as it has visitors descending from the stream of buses that wend their way daily from Lisbon to Sintra.

Centuries before Byron's arrival, Sintra's architects, Nature and Man, unwittingly anticipated the arrival of the age of romanticism. Fecund Nature was properly undisciplined, lacking only a bard to harness the four horsemen of the sensibilities: joy, dread, awe, and wonder. The Serra de Sintra range on the Atlantic coast ensured a preponderance of windswept foggy days. Frenzied streams catapulting down sodden hillsides produced almost impenetrable vegetation. Jagged peaks, dark valleys, deep ravines—Nature's Sintra epitomized the romantic period's enthusiasm for "a setting of natural grandeur cast in a mode of desolation." Sintra was dank, its mountains peaked, its woods mysterious.

Nature's human collaborators had in readiness for Byron's visit the ruins of an eighth-century Moorish castle fourteen hundred feet above sea level. Its crenelated walls etched like jagged teeth on a cliff precipitous enough to deter acrophobics, the castle lacked only a Byronic hero. Captured in 1174 by Alfonso Henriques (the first king of Christian Portugal), the fortress adumbrated romantic structural styles down to the last merlon.

Two religious edifices stood waiting. Atop Sintra's highest peak, the convent of Nossa Senhora de Penha surveyed the coastline, the sweep of the inland plains, and the distant city of Lisbon on the banks of the Tagus. Often cloud enshrouded, the convent featured mists that swirled about it in romantic unpredictability. Nearby, ensconced in the mountainside itself, was the Capuchin or Cork convent, a warren of cork-lined cells carved out of "living rock" (dead rocks are beyond Sintra's purlieus), where through two dark, moldy, cavelike rooms, which in a conventional institution might be called the kitchen and the bathroom, conveniently flowed a natural stream. Convents in Portugal are really monasteries; no one has accused the monks of Sintra of seeking pious seclusion in prosaic settings.

Down in the little town itself, awaiting Byron's arrival stood the royal palace, unchanged even today, with its two monstrous conical chimneys rising from a kitchen area the size of a hockey rink. The rest of the palace, a treasure trove of Portuguese titles (*azulejos*), offered a mélange of architectural styles (a Portuguese specialty of which Sintra had long been an exemplar) incorporating Moorish and Manueline, the latter denoting the transition from Gothic to Renaissance during the reign of Manuel I in the fifteenth century.

At long last, on the morning of July 11, 1809, arrived the man destined to bring Sintra both world attention and a fateful, even neurotic, commitment to the perpetuation of its romantic aura. Byron, in his own way endowed as lavishly by nature as Sintra, came bearing the Janus-like crown of recognition. Sintra responded to the coronation like a beautiful woman whose celebrated charms will drive her to artificial sustenance once they begin to fade.

Byron, at twenty-one, on his first trip away from England had landed in Lisbon on July 2 aboard the packet *Princess Elizabeth*. He rode up to Sintra (or Cintra, as it was then known) nine days later, spending two nights at the local inn. He passed at most three days in the area, one of which was certainly taken up by a trip to the convent and palace at Marfa, twelve miles to the north. In Sintra itself Byron observed the Moorish castle, climbed to the peak of Nossa Senhora de Penha, visited the vacant estate at Monserrate of *Vathek*'s author, William Beckford, sought out the Cork convent, and spent some time in the Marquis de Marialva's Seteais Palace.

Exuberant to be at last in Europe (and possibly avoiding scandal of a homosexual nature in England), filled with excited anticipation at the prospect of the journey that would take him to Greece and Turkey, buoyant with health (he swam the Tagus at Lisbon, a prodigous athletic feat), Byron was captivated by Sintra. Its very excesses matched his exuberance and reflected his spirit. "I must just observe," he wrote from Lisbon to his friend Francis Hodgson on July 16, "that the village of Cintra in Estremadura is the most beautiful, perhaps, in the world." On August 11, he wrote his mother from Gibraltar,

> ... the village of Cintra, about fifteen miles from the capital, is, perhaps in every respect, the most delightful in Europe; it contains beauties of every description, natural and artificial. Palaces and gardens rising in the midst of rocks, cataracts, and precipices; convents on stupendous heights—a distant view of the sea and the Tagus; and, besides (though this is a secondary consideration) is remarkable as the scene of Sir Hew Dalrymple's Convention. It unites in itself all the wildness of the western highlands, with the verdure of the south of France.

Byron had never seen the verdure of the south of France, let alone the rest of Europe. He would soon learn the traveler's penalty for unguarded praise (unable to retract, you are forced to qualify) and on November 12, he wrote his mother from Preveza on the Greek coast: "I then went over the mountains through Zitza, a village with a Greek monastery (where I slept on my return), in the most beautiful situation (always excepting Cintra, in Portugal) I ever beheld."

Sintra was unaware that it had been singled out for praise until almost three years later, when the first two cantos of *Childe Harold's Pilgrimage* were published in March 1812. Childe Harold, the hero of Byron's poem, undertakes a journey whose itinerary is almost precisely that of the poet; Harold visits Sintra as he sets out on his travels. *Childe Harold's Pilgrimage* brought Byron instant celebrity (he took care of his own notoriety), and Sintra was irrevocably persuaded to regard itself as Eden. The heavy municipal burden of perpetuating a vision of one's community as paradise goes beyond the conventional dimensions of civic politics. Sintra resolved to mingle eclectic building and landscaping in a purportedly romantic style with a relentless emphasis on Byron as the celebrant of its heavenly qualities.

In stanza 18 of canto I of *Childe Harold's Pilgrimage*, Byron wrote:

> Lo! Cintra's glorious Eden intervenes
> In variegated maze of mount and glen.
> Ah, me! what hand can pencil guide, or pen,
> To follow half on which the eye dilates
> Through views more dazzling unto mortal ken
> Than those whereof such things the bard relates
> Who to the awe-struck world unlock Elysium's gates?

Following this panegyric, there remained little to do but reinforce the extravagance, and Byron supported his generalities with specifics in stanza 19:

> The horrid crags, by toppling convent crowned,
> The cork-trees hoar that clothe the shaggy steep,
> The mountain-moss by scorching skies imbrowned,
> The sunken glen, whose sunless shrubs must weep,
> The tender azure of the unruffled deep,
> The orange tints that gild the greenest bough,
> The torrents that from cliff to valley leap,
> The vine on high, the willow branch below,
> Mixed in one mighty scene, with varied beauty glow.

W. H. Auden claims that *Childe Harold's Pilgrimage* is unreadable. It is, at any rate, largely unread. "One does not know," Auden writes in his introduction to a volume of

Byron's prose and poetry, "which was the most [sic] disastrous, his choice of hero or his choice of meter." His choice of both hero and meter (iambic-pentameter Spenserian stanzas laden with antiquated rhetoric) met with instantaneous acclaim from Byron's contemporaries.

Byron's creation of a sated and melancholic hero embarking on a pilgrimage in search of himself is difficult to divorce from a fictionalized self-portrait, as he was well aware. The early stanzas of canto I shift narrative perspective back and forth from narrator to Harold, creating a texture that suggests more a lack of design than a complexity of intent. Sometimes Byron forgets Harold altogether. Byron then recalls his hero waiting in the wings, summons him onstage with a belated "So deemed the Childe . . ." and thus asks the reader to reassess many stanzas of what had previously appeared to be the narrator's views.

Byron made a number of factual errors about Sintra. His intent was hardly to offer a precise travel account, but his inaccuracies seem induced by his need to evoke a world steeped in romanticism.

Of the Penha convent, Byron write in stanza 20 of canto I:

> Then slowly climb the many-winding way
> And frequent turn to linger as you go,
> From loftier rocks new loveliness survey,
> And rest ye at "Our Lady's House of Woe . . ."

Byron mistook the Portuguese word *penha* (rock) for *pena* (woe), thus giving a romantic note of despair to a mineral deposit. In the second edition of the poem, Byron notes that Sir Walter Scott had drawn his attention to this error but claimed that he did not think "it necessary to alter the passage . . . as . . . I may well assume the other sense from the severities practised there . . ." thus compounding his error, as the convent was noted for the humane compassion of the monks.

In stanza 21, Byron sees the many crosses bordering the path up to the convent as marking locations of murders committed in a land "where law secures not life." The crosses were, in fact, evidence of the special adoration of the Christian cross that characterized this Hieronymite convent, and had nothing to do with Portuguese mayhem.

Byron's narrator, in whatever guise, observes of Beckford's estate, Monserrate: "There thou, too, Vathek! England's wealthiest son, / Once formed thy Paradise." The narrator goes on to claim that the deserted house, with gaping portals and surrounded by giant weeds, teaches a lesson of vanity and earthly pleasures, an admonition that Beckford, who lived for thirty-two years after *Childe Harold's* triumphant publication, may have thought came from an unlikely source. In truth, the desolate condition of the house resulted from its being untenanted for a decade or so after Beckford's entirely voluntary departure from England.

Childe Harold's Pilgrimage includes a vilification of the Convention of Cintra, a treaty signed in 1808 by the British, French, and Portuguese that allowed the French troops to depart Portugal without penalty. Byron, who thought the treaty a disgraceful travesty of justice, excoriated the "knights in Marialva's dome" as he placed the signing of the treaty in the palatial residence of the Fifth Marquis of Marialva (Beckford's sponsor) in Sintra. In fact, the treaty was negotiated near Torres Vedras and signed in Lisbon. Despite its name, the Convention of Cintra had nothing to do with Sintra, but Byron's error persuaded him to invoke three full stanzas of invective beginning with "Behold the hall where chiefs were late convened!"

The Byron who paid this brief visit to Sintra in 1809 was an excessively handsome young man, a graduate of Harrow and Cambridge, and a poet of modest reputation following the publication of his "English Bards and Scotch Reviewers"; a debtor who owed vast sums at heavy interest against the security of his future and a possible sale of his estate, Newstead; the Seventh Lord Byron, an incumbency he inherited at the age of ten and seems always to have savored, however ironically; a moody, witty, adventurous, incipient traveler who was eager to quit his native country.

"I leave England without regret," he wrote, "I shall return to it without pleasure."

In this century, Byron has attracted almost as many biographer-critics as readers, although his fame appears to have the solidity of Penha's peak. Two of his better critics, Iris Origo and M. K. Joseph, have observed that as a traveler Byron straddled the tradition of the eighteenth-century gentleman on his Grand Tour, and of the middle-class intellectual traveler of the nineteenth century.

On the Grand Tour the well-heeled and frequently titled young man made himself a part of the society of the lands he visited. Travel was then the prerogative of a single class; the aristocratic salons of Europe scarcely recognized national barriers. But as travelers, the nineteenth-century Romantics sought the beauties of nature rather than the pleasures of society; they carried their own world with them, and with few exceptions, felt little need for contacts with the inhabitants of the countries they visited.

This made Sintra an ideal site for Byron.

Byron's first trip abroad was in fact the antithesis of a Grand Tour. He was in his own eyes an adventurer seeking strange and exotic scenes, of which Sintra was the first. He consciously absorbed the atmosphere of foreign sites. But he made numerous human contacts, often, as he was the first to proclaim, on the most intimate level. His interest in nature was as a stage setting, with shifting scenery, on which to enact his own dramas before assigning them to his fictional hero.

An opportunity to assess Byron in this dual light came recently when an adventurous colleague of mine, Maurice

Kasten, persuaded me to seek out Zitza, near Joannina, a site whose beauty Byron had claimed to be second only to Sintra. We climbed to this remote Greek village on the Albanian border and asked the local police representative to direct us to the monastery where Byron had stayed overnight. He told us that if we ventured to continue up the hill ("perhaps there is not in the world a more romantic prospect than that which is viewed from the summit of the hill," Hobhouse had written) we would be shot. By whom, was never made clear. Apart from deep mutual animosity, Greece and Albania were still technically at war with one another, a state that harkens back to World War II. We retreated cravenly to a nearby field for a picnic of peasant bread, feta cheese, and black olives the size of bullets.

This incident gave me a fresh sense of Byron the traveler, who almost two centuries earlier had journeyed from Zitza for nine days deep into Albania where he was received as the guest of Ali Pacha, a grand vizier right out of Beckford's *Vathek*. Byron had a talent for blazing the trail that his fictional heroes would follow.

Immediately following the publication of cantos I and II of *Childe Harold's Pilgrimage*, Byron could well have copyrighted the phrase "overnight fame." Sintra, by extension—how can you improve on Eden?—took on an indelible aura as the quintessentially romantic European location. From that time on, no one could visit, dwell, or build in Sintra without an awareness of Byron's pervasive spirit. Many a castellated atrocity rose in the mistaken impression that Byron's reputation, and that of Sintra, was being embellished.

Sintra's post-Byronic transmogrification was paradoxical. In the immediate vicinity, new structures and gardens were created to evoke a latter-day romanticism. Yet the little town itself was loath to change its 1809 cobblestoned look, which slowly slid from affecting to affectation.

Atop Sintra's highest peak (1,600 feet), the Nossa Senhora

de Penha convent was torn down and replaced by an edifice known today as the Palacio de Pena. It was built in mid-nineteenth century by the consort of Queen Maria II, Ferdinand Saxe-Cooburg-Gotha, a cousin of Queen Victoria's beloved Albert. Of the former convent, he preserved only the Manueline cloister and the chapel. Under his architectural guidance, *penha* inadvertently became *Pena*.

A monument to unbridled eclecticism, the Palacio de Pena is a pseudomedieval baronial castle. The amalgam of discordant architectural styles that went into its creation makes it impossible to take the *palacio* seriously even on its own terms. It has a drawbridge over a waterless moat at the crest of a rockbound summit.

The interior of the Pena palace offers room after eye-popping room of objects that range from rare craftsmanship to unalloyed kitsch. The long formal drawing room boasts a Renaissance coffered ceiling, Moorish fretted walls, and teakwood furniture from India; fretwork plaster panels in pistachio green and birthday-cake pink are lighted by a massive chandelier and four huge *torchères* held by life-size Indian figures.

One of the more intimate salons, the queen's private sitting room, has daunting trompe l'oeil work in sepia and white, with porcelain inlaid furniture. The ribbed vaulted ceiling is set off by doorways shaped in the Moorish horseshoe style. The candelabra, *torchères*, and the chandelier are all made of Saxe china.

When the clouds part and mists dissipate, a transcendent view from the windows, terraces, ramparts, and turrets offers itself as the one truly majestic aspect of the palace. Even Ferdinand couldn't redesign the vista. Lisbon and the Tagus lie to the south, the Colares hills and vineyards—and beyond them the coastline resort of Estoril and Cascais—to the west, the vast sweeping plains of Estremadura to the north and east.

Regarded as a tribute to Byron's celebration of the glories of the site, the Palacio de Pena is a *résidence manqué* whose golden-tiled domes cap a paean to romanticism with orgiastic architectural abandon. Ferdinand's architect was one Baron Eschwege, who for good measure on a nearby peak erected a statue in tribute to himself. He is accoutered as a knight in the armor of the Middle Ages, and it is futile to wish that irony had entered into his self-projection.

Sintra's evocation of Byron's spirit was under way.

He may be counted among the English romantic poets, but Byron was unlikely to write a poem about a daffodil, and violets by a mossy stone were given short shrift. Byron liked nature bold, colorful, and heroic. Nature of this ilk was brought to near-Byronic perfection in mid-nineteenth century on the grounds of Monserrate, four miles southeast of the town. William Beckford's erstwhile residence was transformed between 1846 and 1850 by an English capitalist, Francis Cook. He set out to make Byron's glorious Eden more than a metaphor.

This Monserrate estate, or *quinta*, was first developed by Caetano de Mello e Castro, Viceroy of India, in 1718. He placed his home on a wooded spur in the Serra range amid valleys and streams, with an exceptional view of the distant seacoast. Apart from this line of vision, the entire estate is secluded by the surrounding hills, giving one a sense of remoteness in the midst of nature's extravagant bounty.

William Beckford, who is said to have lived there until 1796, sublet this house two years earlier. Curiously, Robert Southey, an inveterate commentator and sightseer, summering in Sintra in 1796, makes no mention of either Beckford or Monserrate—despite Beckford's fame as a fellow English writer, his notoriety in a sex scandal, and his reputation as the wealthiest man in England. When Byron visited Monserrate in July 1809, he described the estate as "the finest and sweetest spot in this kingdom," and Byron's travel companion, John Hobhouse, declared that "Monserrat [sic] formerly the house of Mr. Beckford, is now devoid of all furniture, and deserted."

The house that stands today at Monserrate appears to have been refurbished by Francis Cook somewhat on the plan of the building that stood there in ruins when he bought the property in 1846. Cook's gardeners created what is really a vast park that still contains thousands of plants and may yet be the finest in all Spain and Portugal. Cook had his landscape artists bring in flora from both Africa and northern Europe. The gardens were laid out with tropical glens and nordic embankments, with cascades, groves of oranges and tangerines, streams, flowering shrubs and exotic blooms in both formal and unstructured beds, cataracts, and in front of the house, a sweeping open lawn whose velvet surface contained minute wildflowers. Thus did Sintra honor Byron's memory.

But is that so? Skeptics might counter that Cook's estate owed nothing to Byron and everything to Cook's imaginative use of his wealth. Tracing the pervasive extent of influence is at best a speculative venture. But Byron's name and image continued unabated as Sintra's arch eulogist, and no literate person could either visit or settle in Sintra without an awareness of Byron's heritage of environmental approval, or, to put it in Cook's terms, his public-relations endowment.

Francis Cook's opulence could scarcely be matched by his Sintra neighbors, but they made a brave effort. Nineteenth-century "Byronic" estates or *quintas*—the word "quinta" here is analogous to the use of "summer cottage" to designate a Newport mansion—all share two features: they are enclosed by high walls and portcullislike entranceways; and their grounds are a riot of giant cork, chestnut, palm, and fir trees, twisting roots, streams, and the occasional bucolic statue. Beyond the encompassing walls, and under the lichen growths on their tiled roofs, are houses colored pink, cream, pale green, yellow, and a favorite—dark rose.

Peasants never lived in Sintra (it was always a residential retreat unsuitable for agronomy and agreeable to royalty) but the influx of the lower classes as servants increased measurably in Byron's wake. Eden may yet turn out to be classless, but Sintra's earthly version of paradise had no truck with democracy, let alone socialism.

Sintra today is really two towns, separated from one another by about half a mile and a quantum esthetic leap. The new town has the railway station, all the appurtenances of a modern Portuguese suburb, and no concern with Byron other than his part in attracting the tourists who pass through en route to the "real" Sintra.

The road leading to the old town follows a parabolic curve on one side of which are rocky projections, pine trees, flowering bushes and vines, and on the other a valley whose floor is a series of cultivated gardens. Modern Sintra is soon out of sight. The old town has kept itself immune from the twentieth century as much as possible. What Byron saw is what we see. Robert Southey's description of Sintra in 1800 is startlingly appropriate today:

> The town is small, like all country towns of Portugal, containing the Plaza or square, and a number of crooked streets that wind down the hill; the palace is old . . . remarkably irregular . . . a large, rambling, shapeless pile . . . two huge connical chimneys, rising incongruously against the landscape . . . [and nearby] summits, and coombs winding to the vale, luxuriantly wooded, chiefly with cork trees . . .

Were it not for today's tourist buses parked row on row before the royal palace, for the taxi stand, and for the souvenir stalls and shops selling postcards with Byron's likeness next to ceramic mugs on which "glorious Eden" is printed beneath a desultory sketch of the palace, this might still be Byron's Cintra. And that is precisely what Sintra hopes to persuade us.

One of Sintra's two churches still lacks a replacement for the steeple felled in the 1755 earthquake that decimated Lisbon. The Tourist Office is new, but its handsome building is two hundred years old. The pavement is cobbled in places— paved roads connected Lisbon and Sintra at least as early as mid-eighteenth century—and village social life still seems to take place largely on the sidewalk.

But Eden is, after all, not a town but a garden, and what attracts travelers who can break away from tour groups is Sintra's natural setting. Perhaps Sintra's greatest boon for today's visitors is that its topographical wonders are accessible. The mountain peaks are climbable and scarcely alpine; the woods and paths never become deep forests; the aerie-palaces are open to the public, albeit on a regimented, paid-admission, and frequently limited basis; and the nearby roads pass through uncommon countryside.

As a Gothic location with subtle undertones of decadence, Sintra may be a little too laden with moss and tangled vines, a trifle too neatly divided between peaks and crags, dark valleys and sun-speckled heaths. Cooler in summer than its neighbors, Sintra predictably specializes in fireflies, not mosquitoes; warmer in winter, Sintra offers abundant fog as a spectral agent of mystery.

Much of the current travel literature on Byron's connection with Sintra is spurious. Publications greedily borrow one another's errors. A favored gaffe is that Byron either began or occupied himself in writing *Childe Harold's Pilgrimage* while he was in Sintra. In reality, Byron began writing the poem on October 31, 1809, three months after he left Sintra. In his own handwriting on the outside cover of the original manuscript of the first two cantos of *Childe Harold's Pilgrimage*, Byron wrote: "Byron—Joannina in Albania, begun

October 31st, 1809. Concluded Canto 2nd, Smyrna, March 28th, 1810. [Signed] BYRON."

One guidebook even claims that "Lord Byron worked on 'Childe Harold' in the front garden" of the Marquis de Marialva's former residence, now the Hotel Palacio dos Seteais. A Michelin green guide on Portugal maintains that "Lord Byron planned *Childe Harold* while at his Sintra inn." What Byron planned, in the absence of any written evidence, is rather difficult to substantiate.

A travel book on Portugal gives directions to this Sintra inn "where Byron lived while producing most of his *Childe Harold*." Two nights is a relatively short time to produce "most of" two hundred stanzas, especially when one's days are taken up with extensive sightseeing. The quotation reveals more about the author of the claim than the author of the poem.

This Sintra inn, once the Hotel Lawrence (named for its English owners) is now the Estalagem dos Cavaleiros. It has a tiled plaque near the entrance reading "Pousada de Lord Byron." When last visited it was closed.

One travel periodical currently published by a major credit card company, wrote that "Lord Byron walked the halls of the Hotel Palacio dos Seteais. From a vantage point above the formal topiary gardens, he peered across patchwork flatlands to the ocean. Turning and looking up, he saw the golden cupolas of the Pena Palace bathed in the dusty light of late afternoon." Byron had been dead a quarter of a century before the Pena palace and its cupolas was built. His ability to turn and look up in the dusty light of a late afternoon at these nonexistent golden cupolas decades prior to their creation warrants rather more attention than a perfunctory paragraph in a travel article.

Perhaps the journalist had recently sampled the Lord Byron Cocktail, created by and currently served in the same Hotel Palacio's elegant bar. This concoction (8/10 Bacardi Rum,

$\frac{1}{10}$ Pisang Ambon, $\frac{1}{10}$ lemon juice, a few drops of Crème de Menthe) seems likely to have won his Lordship's approval more readily than the newsstand souvenir mugs emblazoned with his name and profile.

Sintra's first new hotel in a century, the Tivoli Sintra, has gone up next to the royal palace. From the entranceway, it is reasonably unobtrusive; from across the valley it is an eyesore. But from the inside looking out, a guest has a superb view of Byron's inn and the best of the Sintra countryside. The hotel has four conference rooms, three named for celebrated Portuguese writers, and a fourth, "suitable for meetings, luncheon or dinner, cocktail parties, expositions, and press conferences" is designated the Sala Byron.

In the modest Sintra library, across from the fire station, stands a white marble bust of Lord Byron, now the patron saint of tourism. On the second floor, displayed in a locked glass case, is an early edition of *Childe Harold's Pilgrimage*, opened at the appropriate stanza 18 "glorious Eden" lines, as well as copies of the poem in Portuguese translations.

Of the locations visited by Byron, Monserrate seems to have come full circle. Once more, just as Byron and Hobhouse found it after the occupancy of Beckford, the house is "devoid of all furniture and deserted." The current house is a mammoth structure, two huge neo-Oriental towers separated by galleries at the center of which is a domed square. Peeking through the windows of this exotic and architecturally unclassifiable mansion, one sees elaborate fretwork and carved plaster panels. The vast grounds are now under the supervision of the Portuguese Ministry of Tourism and are open daily for visitors to wander about at will. Despite the occasional direction sign, it is possible to become lost among the cedars, arbutus, bamboos, and bracken.

The Cork convent today has a parking area under nearby trees, one of which has a sign warning visitors to leave no valuables in their parked cars for thieves to rob. Considering that the dark, gloomy cells were constructed in the sixteenth century, and ignoring some contemporary grafitti ("Joao loves Maria"), one still gets an impressive sense of the uncompromising isolation sought by the monks. Twenty-five years after Byron's visit, the Capuchin monks left the convent, claiming that the frequency of visitors (two or sometimes three a month) was making their lives intolerably social.

One building that has nothing to do with romanticism is the Marquis de Marialva's palace, now as the Hotel Palacio dos Seteais one of Europe's most elegant hostelries. It was constructed in 1778 by a diamond millionaire, Daniel Gildemeester, the Dutch consul in Lisbon, whose wife, according to the crisply perceptive William Beckford, had "a dry manner of expressing herself full of spirit and discernment. She is not of the merciful tribe and spares nobody." She may be responsible for the uncompromising restraint of Sintra's single nonromantic and only distinguished architectural structure.

It was here that Byron claimed that the infamous Convention of Cintra was held. Its current name *Sete* (seven) *ais* (sighs) is the Portuguese comment on the treaty. Marialva added a wing to the house in exact replica of the original mansion, and joined the two by a triumphal arch. The house follows classically simple Renaissance lines of harmony, balance, and proportion. Hobhouse wrote that he and Byron were in "the very room in which the famous Convention was signed . . ."

Byron did not invent Sintra, but he changed its image forever. Sintra's tour guides in a wide variety of languages daily invoke Byron's magic name and, remarkably, every tourist seems to know who he is. The magnitude of Byron's fame results not from any single element: not alone from his poetry, which apart from *Don Juan* is little read today, and that largely in academia; not from libidinous reputation despite the notoriety it brought him; not from his heroic death in the cause of Greek freedom; not from his vaunted charisma coupled with his noble rank.

Unlike any other historical figure, in Byron are united Renaissance *and* romantic attributes. Byron lived his life as if it were prescribed by Castiglione's *Courtier* in the fifteenth century; he was aristocrat, militarist, bisexual lover, poet, scholar, revolutionary, adventurer, athlete, politician, and dandy. But to these multifaceted roles he brought the sensibilities of the romantic era: he was a free spirit, although for him that had more do with sexual license than metaphysics; he invested his poetry with original and forthright observation; he exemplified the cult of self as personality; he extolled primitive nature; and he was attracted to medievalism and the exotic in its Oriental-Arabic manifestations

Sintra is not Eden. Indeed, "glorious" is open to serious debate. But Byron, who would become the avatar of the romantic age, seems to have channeled his youthful exuberance and delight in finding himself for the first time in an exotic and foreign milieu by refracting it through his bedazzled consciousness. His pleasure at being away from what he had known all his life, the sights and sounds and mores of England, account for his equating Sintra and Eden.

Byron spent only two nights in Sintra; Sintra's destiny was shaped by his illusion. He spent much of the remainder of his life in Europe. As a sensualist he knew better than to return to Sintra. Paradisiacal visions are not for recapturing.

4

Dostoyevsky's Florence

FYODOR MIKHAILOVICH DOSTOYEVSKY HATED FLORENCE: "I remained stuck so long at Florence only because I had not the money to leave it," he wrote. Most of us leave Florence only because we have not the money to remain. Dostoyevsky and his young second wife, Anna, lived there from late November, 1868, until the following August. He called it hell.

For Dostoyevsky, Florence became the antithesis of those magnetic links that bound Homer and Chaucer to Troy and Proust to Illiers-Combray. Far from using Florence as a literary source, Dostoyevsky wanted only to replace it with St. Petersburg. His repudiation of the city makes mock of conventional platitudes that view Florence as "a source of joy and a fountain of knowledge for the countless visitors that [arrive] every year . . . a special kind of haven, a place of inspiration for some of the greatest literary figures of all time . . ." Dostoyevsky found Florence a source of woe and an empty reservoir, a special kind of purgatory, entirely bereft of inspiration.

Florentine legends spring from municipal self-assurance

61

sustained by past centuries of accolades. "One of the greatest of all novels, Dostoyevsky's *The Idiot*, was written in Florence in 1868 and 1869," writes a Florentine historian. Nonsense. *The Idiot* is not one of the greatest of all novels, nor was it written in Florence. *The Idiot* is a major Dostoyevsky novel whose revised final chapters were in the publishers' hands less than two months after Dostoyevsky's arrival.

In addition to hell, Dostoyevsky ranked Florence below the site of his eight years in prison and exile. "In Florence," he claimed, "there are lacking many advantages which even in Siberia, as soon as I left prison, made themselves evident to me."

Under optimum conditions—an unlikely state for Dostoyevsky, implying a release from poverty, recurrent attacks of epilepsy, and his self-imposed exile to escape his Russian creditors—Florence was not a city to warrant his enthusiasm. A confirmed Slavophile, he believed Russia's future lay with the people and their land, not in emulating Europe. Russia moved directly from the Middle Ages to the nineteenth century adroitly bypassing the Renaissance. Florence epitomized the Renaissance; as such it had nothing to say to Dostoyevsky.

On my first visit to Florence I had no idea that Dostoyevsky had lived there. I was aware only that he had spent some time away from Russia after publishing *Crime and Punishment*. The Norton Critical Edition of that novel notes that in 1868–69 Dostoyevsky lived abroad—in "Germany and Switzerland." Italy is nowhere mentioned, let alone Florence. Not that Dostoyevsky's stay in Italy was a secret; my discovery of his sojourn in Florence was entirely one of replacing personal ignorance with readily available information.

Thus when I came upon a Florentine building that claimed to have served as a residence for Dostoyevsky I thought it suspect. I had crossed the Ponte Vecchio, making my way along the overcrowded Via Guicciardina toward the Pitti

Palace, when a four-story dwelling caught my eye. Near the entranceway, a small plaque noted Dostoyevsky's residence where, it claimed, in 1869 he wrote his novel, *The Idiot*. I didn't believe it.

I altered my day's schedule. Instead of the Pitti Palace I went to one of the city's tourist offices. There I encountered a woman whose sole object in life appeared to be repudiation of any traveler who entered her precincts. In a city where tourism is often close to frenetic, she had developed an antipathy toward tourists that expressed itself in a condescension so overpowering it would intimidate a German tour guide.

"*Mamma mia!*" she exclaimed (an expression I thought confined to low-budget Italian films). "Of course Dostoyevsky lived and wrote there. Everyone knows that. Do you think perhaps that Florence puts up plaques to cover holes in the plaster? Do you consider that the Tourist Bureau is in the business of having to verify what every intelligent person knows? Are you perhaps making treasonable assertions about the integrity of the municipality?"

By this time I had backed myself cravenly to the door, and found the narrow sidewalk under my feet. She was still expostulating as I rounded the corner. I decided to do what I should have undertaken in the first place; check the biographical record. But before that I walked sheepishly toward the Pitti Palace, glancing sidelong at Dostoyevsky's building on my right. Just a block away was the Casa Guidi, the home of the nineteenth century's celebrated lovers, Elizabeth Barrett and Robert Browning. Is it possible to conceive of a city block on which Elizabeth Barrett Browning and Fyodor Mikailovich Dostoyevsky dwelled as neighbors? Despite the Tourist Office lady, not bloody likely.

But I was wrong, give or take a decade and a slanting of the facts.

In 1867 Dostoyevsky left Russia with his bride, twenty-five

years his junior, ostensibly on a trip of three months. He and Anna Grigorevna remained abroad over four years.

Dostoyevsky gave two reasons for the trip: ". . . In the first place I had to save my health and even my life. The attacks [of epilepsy] were recurring every eight days, and it was unbearable to feel and recognize the destruction of my nerves and brain. I really was beginning to lose my senses, that is a fact. I felt it; the ruin of my nerves often drove me to the very edge of things. The second reason is that my creditors would wait no longer, and on the day of my departure several summonses were out against me . . ."

Second reasons frequently turn out to be first imperatives. Not only was Dostoyevsky seeking to escape debtor's prison, but also to avoid those who were in debt to him. His widowed sister-in-law, her children, and particularly his stepson, Paul, all plagued him to assume their expenses. Importunity was one of those moral pressures likely to find a Dostoyevsky who submitted weakly—or triumphed spiritually—depending on one's viewpoint. His bride was of the former opinion.

She persuaded him to let her dowry cover the expenses of the trip.

"I loved Fyodor Mikhailovich without limit," she wrote in her *Reminiscences*, "but this was not a physical love, not a passion which might have existed between persons of equal age. My love was entirely cerebral. It was an idea existing in my head. It was more like adoration and reverence for a man of such talent and such novel qualities of spirit. It was a searing pity for a man who had suffered so much without ever knowing joy and happiness.

"All that," she admitted, "was exalted feelings, dreams which could be crushed by the onset of harsh reality." Nevertheless, ". . . the dream of becoming his life's companion, of sharing his labors and lightening his existence, of giving him happiness—that was what took hold of my imagination; and Fyodor Mikhailovich became my God, my idol."

A woman who offers her life to a man as compensation for his past is a loaded revolver about to misfire. But Anna Grigorevna hit the bull's eye.

Sharing quarters with a man for more than half a year in a city which he hated brought that "harsh reality" to challenge her determination to lighten his existence. During their marriage of almost two years they had endured much together, and Anna knew that Florence, despite their poverty and inability to move away, was not a permanent situation. When Dostoyevsky railed against their existence in Florence, Anna was aware that by his own admission her husband had "never been acquainted with moderation." But this very lack of moderation was the source of his literary strength. She knew that, too. "In all things I go to the uttermost extreme," Dostoyevsky confessed disarmingly of his private life and prophetically of his artistic potential.

The trip began badly. In Germany, Dostoyevsky gambled away their funds and Anna was forced to pawn her wedding present of a diamond-and-ruby brooch and earrings. "Lost forever," she wrote cryptically. Her forebearance, his suffering ("he would start sobbing, fall on his knees before me and beg my forgiveness for torturing me with his behavior. He would fall into utter despair. . .") should remind those critics who object to melodramatic scenes in Dostoyevsky's novels that they often recapitulate his own domestic life.

Finally they received an advance from the editor of the *Russian Messenger*. They went to Geneva, a city that proved a forerunner of Florence. Dostoyevsky found the city "detestable . . . the essence of tedium." He began work on *The Idiot*. Anna Grigorevna saw the frequent weather changes as having "an oppressive effect on Fyodor Mikhailovich's nerves and his epileptic seizures grew much more frequent." Anna herself was pregnant. They lived in poverty. On February 22, 1868, their daughter Sonya was born. She was Dostoyevsky's first child. She lived only three months, and her death cast her parents into a depression that they hoped might be alleviated somewhat if they left Geneva and moved south to Vevey.

"In all the fourteen years of our married life I cannot recall a summer more wretched than the one my husband and I spent in Vevey in 1868," wrote Anna Grigorevna. In September they left for Milan. Autumn in Milan was rainy and cold. The reading rooms had neither Russian books nor Russian newspapers. After two months they moved to Florence "for the winter."

Florence was as cold as Milan, as wretched as Vevey, as detestable as Geneva. "The climate of Florence," wrote Dostoyevsky in late January on 1869, "is perhaps even more unfavorable to my health than that of Milan or Vevey; the epileptic attacks return more frequently. Two, within an interval of six days. Besides, it rains too much in Florence . . . for a fortnight it was somewhat cool, and as the houses were poorly equipped, we froze during that fortnight like mice in a cellar."

Dostoyevsky and his wife were living in the building on the Via Guicciardini near the Pitti Palace. Even today, despite steam heat and modern comforts, January in Florence can be a rain-swept, chilling experience. For Dostoyevsky, living in poverty, it was miserable.

One positive note was the availability of Russian newspapers in the Florence library. Every day after dinner Dostoyevsky went there to read the two Russian periodicals held on subscription. He borrowed the works of Voltaire and Diderot for his winter reading at home. For six months prior to his arrival in Florence, Dostoyevsky had not seen a single Russian newspaper. He was starved for news of home.

But his was not merely the heightened interest of all travelers in reading about their homeland in a familiar periodical. The core of Dostoyevsky's being was Russia. The themes, the ideas, the characters, the settings, the dialogue, and the philosophical overtones of all Dostoyevsky's work are almost preternaturally Russian. He thought of himself as having a Russian soul. Away from Russia, he felt stripped of his creative sources.

Almost two years separation from his home country found Dostoyevsky "lacking fresh Russian impressions." He found it "difficult . . . to write anything at all . . ." "I cannot write here," he wrote from Florence to his niece Sonya. "For that I must be in Russia without fail, must see, hear, and take direct part in Russian life; whereas here I am losing even the possibility of writing, since I lack both the essential material, namely Russian reality (which produces the ideas) and the Russian people."

Anna Grigorevna writes in her *Reminiscenses* that not only Russian people but people in general were lacking. "We did not know a single soul in Florence with whom we could argue, talk, joke, exchange reactions. Around us, all were strangers, and sometimes hostile ones; and this total isolation from people was sometimes difficult to bear." In Russia Dostoyevsky was a celebrated author; in Florence he was nobody. Or rather, he was a gaunt and bearded impoverished foreigner, speaking not a word of Italian, subject to sudden frightening epileptic attacks.

For Dostoyevsky and his wife, the nine months spent in Florence necessarily lent themselves to different perspectives. She wrote about Florence decades later, after Dostoyevsky's death in 1881, and she used her notebooks and diary for research to support her memory. In the latter part of her life she made a major contribution to Dostoyevsky scholarship. She lived for thirty-seven years after his death, and died at the time of the 1917 Russian Revolution.

She was at pains to present her "idol" as a man not entirely indifferent to the artistic wealth of Florence, despite contrary evidence. Hell, let alone Siberia, is not generally thought of as a place that includes the Uffizi and the Bargello, the Academy and the Piazza della Signorini,the San Lorenzo Library and the Duomo.

Anna Grigorevna recalls her husband's "ecstatic reaction to the Cathedral, the Church of Santa Maria del Fiore, and the small Chapel dei Battistero . . . the bronze doors of the Baptistry . . . the work of the renowned Ghiberti, enchanted my husband, and passing the Chapel often, he always stopped to look at them." Often, she wrote, they walked across the street to the Pitti Palace, where Dostoyevsky was "entranced by Raphael's painting, Madonna della Sedia." They visited the Uffizi Museum as well, and once again Dostoyevsky was said to be "enchanted."

"Enchantment," "ecstasy," and "entrancement" may well have been Dostoyevsky's reaction to the art of Florence, but they are entirely absent from his letters written at the time. Great art may serve to warm, refresh, and revive, but Dostoyevsky remained cold and miserable. Florence was only part of a larger canvas of travel outside Russia. Just being abroad was "worse than deportation to Siberia. I mean that quite seriously; I'm not exaggerating." In March he wrote from Florence that "Life abroad becomes more unbearable to me every day."

Whether or not the artistic wealth of Florence "entranced" him, what he wrote about was the repellent weather, a concern that became an obsession. ". . . The guide books say that Florence, by reason of its position, is the coldest town in winter in all Italy." In summer they rented a "tiny dwelling." Florence now became "the hottest town in the whole peninsula, and even in the whole Mediterranean region— only some parts of Sicily and Algiers," wrote Dostoyevsky, who had been to neither location, "can touch Florence for heat. Well, and so it was hot as hell, and we bore it like true Russians, who notoriously can bear anything."

The money they had been expecting did not arrive, and they had to stay "in that hole (where we caught two beastly tarantulas) three whole months." Neither he nor his wife give the precise location of "that hole" but it appears to have been in the building facing what is now known to visitors as the Straw Market. This market, the Loggia di Mercato Nuovo, was built in 1551 by Battista del Tasso for Cosimo I as headquarters for the Guild of Bankers and Money Changers. The site has four massive pillars supporting an arcade whose columned aisles terminate in symmetrical groined vaults.

"In the square," wrote Dostoyevsky, "was a municipal fountain in the form of a gigantic bronze boar from whose throat the water flowed (It is a classic masterpiece of rare beauty.)" Tourists today rub the boar's snout, now shiny from incessant attention, and throw coins in the dry well for luck.

But for Dostoyevsky the market square was characterized mainly by insufferable heat. ". . . reflect that all those arcades and masses of stone by which the whole square is surrounded, drank in and accumulated all the heat of the sun, and got as scorching as a stove pipe in a vapour bath—and that was the atmosphere we lived in. The real heat, that is, the real hell-heat, we had to groan under for six weeks (earlier, it was just in a sort of way endurable)."

The frustrations and torments of his stay in Florence seemed to persuade Dostoyevsky that extremes in weather were a geographical peculiarity that bypassed Russia. But as he well knew, winter in Florence is balmy compared to that season in St. Petersburg; and many summer days there can offer Florence torrid competition. Before setting out on this trip he had written in *Crime and Punishment* of midsummer in St. Petersburg: "The heat in the streets was stifling. The stuffiness, the jostling crowds, the bricks and mortar, scaffolding and dust everywhere, and that peculiar summer stench so familiar to everyone who cannot get away from St. Petersburg into the country . . ." In another passage he writes of St. Petersburg that "the heat was still as oppressive" and the streets were filled with the "dusty, foul-smelling, contaminated air of the town."

"Try to depict to yourself," Dostoyevsky wrote Sonya, "what we in Florence, during the whole of June and July, and half of August, were going through! In my whole life I've never experienced anything like it!" When Dostoyevsky had written of the summer discomforts of St. Petersburg in *Crime and Punishment*, the perspective had been that of Raskolnikov, his tormented protagonist. "The heat outside was again overpowering; not so much as a drop of rain had fallen all this time. Again the same dust and bricks and mortar, the stinking shops and public houses, the drunkards everywhere, the Finnish hawkers, the broken-down old cabs."

Unlike Raskolnikov, Dostoyevsky had not murdered anyone, but his torment was as real as that of his protagonist: his searing poverty, exacerbated by his guilt at gambling away all of Anna's funds, his illness, and his anxiety at being unable to write were provocation enough to make his refracted view of Florence analogous with Raskolnikov's view of St. Petersburg. In both cases, the images of the cities of their torment passed from the "medium" of the actual city through their anguished imaginations to that of a city obliquely perceived as a reflection of the psyche. Florence was not hell. Dostoyevsky's life while living there was hell.

In addition to insupportable weather, Florence, according to Dostoyevsky, had a population that never went to bed. "The population of Florence spends the whole night on its feet, and there's a terrible deal of singing. Of course we had our windows open at night; then about five o'clock in the morning, the people began to racket in the market, and the donkeys to bray, so that we could never close an eye." And in Raskolnikov's St. Petersburg: "Terrible despairing wails rose shrilly to his ears from the street below; they were, however, only what he was used to hearing from his window between two and three o'clock in the morning."

Dostoyevsky's inability to work in Florence was real enough. Less than a month after he left Florence for Dresden he wrote:

I must absolutely deliver the beginning of my novel [*The Possessed*] for the January [1870] number of *Roussky Viestnik*. Moreover, I took an advance of three hundred roubles from the *Sarya* early in the year, and that with a promise to send them this very year a story of at least three sheets. At the present moment I have not begun either the one or the other of these tasks; at Florence I could not work on account of the heat.

This anguished incapacity made Dostoyevsky reflect on what for him were its omnipresent companions, poverty and illness. Of his impecunious despair in Florence he wrote:

It was stupid of me to run away to foreign lands; assuredly 'twere better to have stayed at home and let myself be put in the debtor's prison. Those cursed creditors will kill me for a certainty ... If we had not been able to borrow two hundred francs from an acquaintance, and to get a further hundred from other sources, we might easily have died of hunger in this foreign town. But what worried us most was the constant suspense and uncertainty.

His illness was another torment. The first of Dostoyevsky's epileptic attacks appears to have taken place when he was in his twenties. He was persecuted and burdened by them for the rest of his life. True to his habit of incorporating autobiographical elements in his fiction, he made epilepsy a vital issue in the drama of old man Karamazov's death at the hands of the epileptic, Smerdyakov. Within the vast sweep of

The Brothers Karamazov, Dostoyevsky used his painful knowledge of epilepsy to enrich an ingenious plot.

After he left Florence, Dostoyevsky looked back on his physical condition there and commented that "Florence was extraordinarily beneficial to my health, and even more so to my nerves . . . It was precisely on the *hottest* days that epilepsy was least perceptible, and my attacks in Florence were much slighter than anywhere else." But when living in Florence he had claimed precisely the opposite: the city's climate he declared unfavorable to his health; the frequent recurrence of the epileptic attacks he cited as two within a period of six days. Dostoyevsky had a tendency to view the past more favorably than the present; when in Florence, Siberia seemed preferable; once having left Florence, the excoriated heat metamorphosed into a physiological benefit.

Anna Grigorevna emerges as a model of concern and understanding in dealing with Dostoyevsky's epilepsy. She maintained a lifelong vigil to avoid when possible circumstances that would upset Dostoyevsky's nervous system. Soon after her marriage, she, an inexperienced girl of twenty who had never witnessed an epileptic fit, was left alone (as everyone had fled the room in horror) with her stricken husband writhing and frothing at the mouth in an attack of exceptional severity. Terrified though she was, she tried vainly to keep him from falling, and then supported his head as he slipped to the floor.

She was pregnant during much of their stay in Florence, and a daughter, Lyubov (love) was born to them in Dresden in September 1869. They had gone to Dresden, as, according to Anna, they deemed it "necessary to move to a country where French and German was spoken, so that my husband could talk freely with the doctor, the midwife, the shopkeepers and so forth." In Florence, she "learned to speak a little Italian—that is, enough to speak to the servant or go to the shops. I could even read the newspapers . . . and understood everything." Not so for Dostoyevsky. "Fyodor Mikhailovich, engrossed in his own work, could not learn the language, of course, and I served as his translator." The man who by his own admission found it impossible to work in Florence would be neither the first nor the last traveler to assert his animosity toward a distasteful environment by repudiating its language.

Dostoyevsky is scornful of visitors to Florence from foreign lands who seemed inexplicably to enjoy a city he found intolerable.

> What astonished me most—me, who was imprisoned in Florence by untoward circumstance—was that of the itinerant foreigners (who are nearly all very rich) most remained in Florence; new ones even arrived every day ... when I saw in the streets well-dressed Englishwomen and even French women, I could not conceive *why those who had money to get away with*, could voluntarily stay in such a hell.

Dostoyevsky's repudiation of Florence is tellingly unlike that of another repudiator, Mark Twain, who visited the city briefly just a year before Dostoyevsky. Twain dismissed Florence because of the undemocratic framework of what he considered the religion-oppressed art sovereignty of a beggar-ridden city. In contrast to Twain, Dostoyevsky takes for granted the church as a dominant cultural and social force; the beggars on the other hand were as likely to think of him as one of their own as not.

In line with his characteristic detachment generated by retrospection, Dostoyevsky in his 1877 *Diary of a Writer* recalled those two beastly tarantulas he claimed to have snared in that hole of a Florentine apartment. A decade had reduced the tarantulas to one only, and its demise takes place at the hands of maidservants. "In the opinion of the

Italians, in summer Florence is the hottest—and in winter the coldest—city in all Italy. . . . In the month of July in the apartment which I rented from a landlord, an alarm went out: all of a sudden two maidservants, led by the mistress, burst into my room—they had just seen a *piccola bestia* running into my room from the corridor outside; it had to be killed by all means. *Piccola bestia* is a tarantula."

Although Dostoyevsky's letters in 1868–69 give the impression that he was visiting Florence for the first time, he had been there in 1862 on his first trip outside Russia. He writes in *Winter Notes on Summer Impressions*: "I was in Berlin, in Dresden, in Wiesbaden, in Baden-Baden, in Cologne, in Paris, in London, in Lucerne, in Geneva, in Genoa, in Florence, in Milan, in Venice, in Vienna, and in some of these places twice—and all this I toured in just about two and a half months." He knew that with such an itinerary he could examine nothing in detail, but hoped that "out of all these precious things there will be formed some sort of whole, some sort of general panorama. All the 'land of holy wonders' will present itself to me at once, in a bird's eye view, like the promised land and in perspective from a mountain top."

This first visit to Florence is described by Avrahm Yarmolinsky in his *Dostoyevsky, Words and Days*:

In Geneva he met Strakhov [philosopher, critic, ingrained Slavophile, Dostoyevsky's lifelong friend] and the two went on to Florence, spending a leisurely week there. They walked into the Uffizi, and, despite Strakhov's protests, promptly walked out again. Except for the Madonna de la Sedia, Dostoyevsky was bored by the canvases. The other monuments of the city meant no more to him. He was interested above all in the new faces that he saw about him, the private conflicts that he could read into them. He had no eyes for landscape and cared little for the sights of the town except as a backdrop for the human drama. They spent the days walking the streets where the crowd was thickest, and in the evening they would sit over a glass of local red wine and talk.

In this very indifference as a conventional tourist lay one of Dostoyevsky's strengths as an artist. Landscapes and settings were backgrounds for human drama in his novels. The minds and hearts of his characters constituted the real places of interest, the equivalent of starred sites for exceptional vistas. The St. Petersburg of *Crime and Punishment*, meticulously and even hauntingly evoked, underscores the metaphysical environment adumbrating Raskolnikov's fate. The city is the novel's Greek chorus.

The bird's-eye view of Europe that Dostoyevsky sought on this first European trip established an adversarial attitude that found confirmation in his two later European trips. Western Europe was what Ivan Karamazov called "a graveyard." Dostoyevsky found Europe bourgeois in the worst sense of the term; he excoriated European cities and people alike; he denounced "Westerners" such as his compatriot Turgenev. The future of Russia lay within its boundaries and not in political or social emulation of its Western neighbors. God knows how he would have dealt with America. As Svidrigaylov is about to shoot himself in *Crime and Punishment* he likens his suicidal "journey" to a trip to America. And Svidrigaylov is not a man who believes in paradise, but one who speculates that eternity might well be "like a bathhouse in the country, black with soot, with spiders in every corner . . ."

Dostoyevsky's emphatic repudiation of Florence is mirrored by this larger view of Europe and Europeans. Here speaks a man not given to moderation: "Paris is the most boring city . . . the French, with God as my judge, are enough to make a man nauseated;" Geneva is a "dull, gloomy, stupid town with a frightful climate" whose "winds bring with them the chill of eternal ice." Berlin is "tedious", Milan is "rainy and expensive"; Rome is "too hot"; Dresden, "too cold." The Germans "get on my nerves" and "are all usurers, rascals and cheats!" No one escapes. Not the English, nor the Italians, and above all, not the Swiss, whose Alpine peaks and shimmering lakes are reduced to mundane picture-postcard settings for stodgy people who personify the term *ennui.*

Florence as hell is a peculiarly Dostoyevskian conceit. He is oblivious to the recognition of a city that embodies the spirit of the Western world's greatest cultural revolution. He was "stuck" there in creative and material deprivation. He longed only to escape. He invented a Florence that reflected his psyche. If the degree of obliquity of vision determines the incidence of refraction, then Dostoyevsky's perspective of Florence was close to horizontal. The Florence that passed through the prism of his imagination resembles a ray of narcissistic light. His Florence becomes a self-portrait.

5

Irving's Alhambra

WASHINGTON IRVING INVENTED THE ALHAMBRA. HIS model was a ruinous site that in time came to resemble his romantic conception of its former grandeur. Irving's reputation on its own had scarcely enough clout to dent, let alone alter, a mammoth historic site such as the Alhambra palaces in Spain's Granada. His book, *The Alhambra*, did it all.

Unlike Byron with his fleeting visit to Sintra, Irving lived within the Alhambra palace complex for three months in 1829. The astonishing fact is that Irving's name is now linked with the Alhambra at least as prominently as those of the Arabic and Spanish rulers whose royal residence it was. Where Byron mentioned Sintra in passing as the ideal romantic site for his peripatetic hero, Irving made the Alhambra the romantic centerpiece of his entire book.

Irving's image of the Alhambra at the height of its Arabic glory became a literal reality. Weaving together forty-four chapters of myth, legend, and occasional fact, Irving brought international attention to the Moorish fortress-palace. He altered and shaped its future.

The Alhambra electrified the nineteenth-century reading public. Edition after edition, translation after translation, the book made the Alhambra a world-famous site. Today, the Alhambra's administrators and guides rank Irving as the single most important influence in making the site universally recognized.

Irving was forty-six years old when he lived in the Alhambra. Born in New York City, the youngest of eleven children, he achieved early recognition with his burlesque *History of New York*, and in 1919, with his *Sketch Book* containing tales of Rip Van Winkle and Sleepy Hollow. In 1826 he was attached to the American Legation in Madrid where he researched (some say translated) his life of Columbus and his *Chronicle of the Conquest of Granada*. In 1828 he lived in Seville.

On May 1, 1829, Irving set out from Seville for Granada and the Alhambra with Prince Dmitri Ivanovitch Dolgorouki, a member of the Russian embassy at Madrid. The horseback journey through rugged mountain passes often infested by robbers took several days; overnight accommodation was miserably primitive.

Irving was familiar with the rigors and hardships of such travel. But his need to clothe his experience in sentimental rhetoric caused him to refer to this brief trip with Dolgorouki as "wandering together among the romantic mountains of Andalusia." They were not wandering, but heading directly for Granada; the romantic aspect of the mountains is moot and assuredly subjective. The distinction between the actual journey and Irving's observations presciently suggest something of the literary treatment he would bring to his book on the Alhambra.

The governor of the Province of Granada, on whom Irving called this first week in May, offered his Alhambra suite to Irving and Dolgorouki. Thus Irving, a few days after his arrival in Granada, began his three-month Andalusian sojourn as a resident of the Alhambra itself. The Alhambra, high on a promontory above the city, was really a small fortress town. Apart from the extensive contiguous Moorish palaces with their many rooms, courtyards, and gardens, there was the colossal sixteenth-century Renaissance palace built by Charles V, as well as a scattering of houses and shops, a Franciscan convent, and a parochial church.

This Alhambra of May 1829, had suffered years of neglect and decay. But instead of dismay at the condition of his chosen subject, Irving knew instinctively that he had plumbed a rich literary ore.

The Arabic palace had all the characteristics of the quintessential romantic site, a veritable roll call of the components of romanticism in the early nineteenth century: a decaying ruin evoking much of its original architectural grandeur; an historical backdrop of the Moslem East and the medieval-Renaissance-Christian West; bygone residents whose adventurous lives were waiting to be brought to biographical life; a heterogeneous group of "common" people, then in residence, ripe with anecdotal legend and myth; and a landscape of dramatic natural beauty.

Best of all for Irving, he had the freedom of body and spirit to wander at will through these gardens and buildings. He saw them as the exotic province of diverse cultures about which, in the past three years in Spain, he had become an enthusiastic exponent.

Irving maintained that "the more proudly a mansion has been tenanted in the day of its prosperity, the humbler are its inhabitants in the day of its decline, and the palace of the king commonly ends in being the nesting-place of the beggar." The Alhambra of 1829 amply supported this observation.

The Alhambra was then guarded by a handful of invalid soldiers living in a nearby garrison. Along with these token defenders and a housekeeping family in residence, the compound was a riot of unconventional tenancy. Whenever a tower fell to decay, it was seized by what Irving called "some tatterdemalion family who became joint tenants with the bats and owls of its golden halls and hang their rags, those standards of poverty, out of its windows and loopholes."

Irving's fellow tenants found other unlikely quarters in and about the palace. In a hovel built of reeds and plaster just above the iron entrance gate lived Irving's self-appointed guide and purveyor of myth and legend, the ubiquitous Mateo Ximines and his family. In a closet under the outer staircase lived an old woman, Maria Antonia Sabonea, who had reputedly buried five husbands "and a half . . ." The half was a young dragoon who had expired during courtship, but this Spanish equivalent of Chaucer's Wife of Bath was alive and flourishing as Irving's neighbor. In a vaulted room beneath the Hall of the Ambassadors, a confined maniac, the brother of the housekeeper's aunt, rent the night air with shrieks and howls. Irving was being treated to a preview of Poe's House of Usher.

Unconfined, and strutting about the premises, was an old man with an ample paunch and a bottle nose, wearing a cocked hat of oilskin with a red cockade, proclaiming his noble descent to all who would listen. In fair weather, atop one of the towers, a lean fellow maneuvered two or three fishing rods. His hooks were baited with flies as he attempted to catch the swallows and marlets nesting and flying about. "The angler in the sky," as Irving dubbed him, was merely one of a group of the "Sons of the Alhambra" who took up fishing posts from various vantage points.

No casting call was necessary. Irving's characters were already on stage waiting for him.

Not only humans shared these palatial quarters. Cats (then as now) roamed the Alhambra at will; at night they fought, howled, and mated, often simultaneously. Bats swooped in and out of casements, through arcades and arches, darting past the turrets, sleeping in the cool darkness of the elegant tiled chambers of the royal baths. "A stately peacock," writes Irving, "and his hen seem to hold sway over pompous turkeys, querulous guinea fowls and a rabble rout of cocks and hens."

Irving's fellow tenants in the Alhambra were another link in the literary chains of peasants, village girls, innkeepers, eccentric rustics, and domestic animals that had brought him his greatest success ten years before. What was once the local color of the Hudson Valley was now suffused with the luminous tropical sunlight of the Andalusian spring.

But when it suited his purpose, Irving conceived of himself as being entirely alone. Casting himself in the role of the solitary dreamer, he seemed at ease in writing:

> I feel as if living in one of the enchanted palaces that we used to read of in the Arabian Nights. I wander by day and night through great halls, all decorated with beautiful reliefs and with Arabic inscriptions, that have stood for centuries; through open courts, and with fountains and flowers, where there is every thing assembled to delight the senses, yet where there is not a living being to be seen.

Drugged by his own rhetoric, Irving may even have believed such passages when he wrote them. By his own evidence, not only were there plenty of living things to be seen, but the "beautiful reliefs . . . and Arabic inscriptions" were frequently "scrawled over"—as Irving noted elsewhere—and the Alhambra was at the mercy of "the pilferings of the tasteful traveler." Prince Dolgorouki echoed this view: "Many travelers, wishing to perpetuate their visit to the Alhambra, have marred its walls, covering them with their names and thoughts."

Irving unabashedly claimed accuracy for his description of the palace complex: "Everything in [*The Alhambra*] relating to myself and to the actual inhabitants of the Alhambra is unexaggerated fact," he wrote.

He did not claim accuracy for his historical account—on the contrary he acknowledged that he was weaving a legendary mythic web: "it was only in the legends that I indulged in *romancing*," he wrote a friend. In *The Alhambra* Irving traced the history of the site from its earliest days to the moment of his arrival.

A palace suggests the residence of a sovereign, but James Dickie, critic and art historian, warns us that the term is inappropriate for the Alhambra. "The Alhambra," he writes,

> reveals itself as a complex of buildings designed to house a complexity of functions. It was the seat of government; it housed an army and much else besides. In the Alhambra were to be found not only civil and military zones but an entire *medina*: commercial, administrative and even industrial quarters, all in addition to six palaces, several mosques and a mausoleum.

Two notable elements in Irving's "legendary" history of the Alhambra are his view of Boabdil, the last Arab monarch to occupy the Alhambra, and his attitude toward the French occupancy of the Alhambra during the Napoleonic Peninsular Wars.

Boabdil, or El Rey Chico (the boy king), is generally viewed by historians as a weak man who preferred banishment by Ferdinand and Isabella in 1492 to bloody confrontation. For Irving, Boabdil emerges as a romantic victim of circumstances. Irving's identification with Boabdil often led him to imagine himself as the monarch strolling through the halls of the palaces. Psychohistorians have a ready-made analysand in Irving, whose chosen link with the irresolute and ultimately defeated Boabdil tells more about the American than the legendary Arab. Irving's biographer-critics castigate him for the very qualities attributed to Boabdil, even to Irving's indecision over his departure from the Alhambra (Irving reigned for only three months).

"Of all the necessities of life, Irving most disliked difficult decisions," writes Stanley Williams, whose exhaustive two-volume critical biography is indispensable to Irving scholarship despite its author's patronizing tone. Williams finds Irving exasperating. He wants Irving to be someone else. He wishes Irving's writing were better, his character stronger, and vice versa. As if encouraging him to a sense of responsibility, Williams keeps admonishing Irving (long since laid to rest in his grave with due honors before Williams's critique), exhorting him to greater efforts. Williams sounds like a petulant college professor (he taught at Yale) advising a student whose themes never quite realize their potential.

Williams believed that Irving should not have left the Alhambra after three months. He should have remained there. "It is easy to believe that, had he done so, his more ambitious hopes for his writing might have been realized." At the time of Irving's departure, *The Alhambra* was a jumble of notes except for a few essays. "He could easily have used another six months in the Alhambra, carrying out his intention of making these essays 'bear the stamp of real intimacy with the charming scenes described.' " Worldwide recognition of *The Alhambra* suggests that Irving may have found the stamp regardless.

When Irving's alter-ego Boabdil left the Alhambra fortress for exile, he requested that the gate used by him be closed up with stones, never to be reopened. Looking back, Boabdil "uttered his last sorrowful exclamation." It was here that Boabdil's mother spoke the apocryphal "you do well to weep as a woman over what you could not defend as a man." Irving's assessment of Boabdil is strikingly a list of qualities that some critics attribute to Irving himself:

He gives evidence of a mild and amiable character. He
... won the hearts of his people by his affable and
gracious manners; he was always placable ... He was
personally brave; but he wanted moral courage; and in
times of difficulty and perplexity, was wavering and
irresolute.

Williams continues his adjudication of Irving: "He should
have stayed to finish *The Alhambra*. But such a stand would
have been an anomaly in Irving's character.... When he
abandoned the law and turned writer and wandered, he cast
in his lot with those who look with skepticism on the rigor-
ous conduct of life."

"How easy it is," says Irving in context with Boabdil, for
those who come later "to preach heroism" over matters they
have not experienced.

The other provocative historical element is Irving's view of
the French occupancy of the Alhambra (c. 1811):

When Granada was in the hands of the French, the
Alhambra was garrisoned by their troops ... and occa-
sionally inhabited by the French commander. With that
enlightened taste which has ever distinguished the French
nation in their conquests, this monument of Moorish
elegance and grandeur was rescued from the absolute
ruin and desolation that were overwhelming it.

The Spanish disagree. The editor of an English edition of
The Alhambra printed in Granada in 1979 writes:

This was far from being the case. The French commander,
prior to evacuating the Alhambra, mined it and would
have blown it up but for the presence of mind of a
Spanish ex-soldier who cut the fuse. The depredations of
Napoleon's troops in Spain are a shocking episode in the

history of war, exceeded only by the barbarities inflicted on the civil population . . .

Irving maintains that "Spain may thank her [French] invaders for having restored to her the most beautiful and interesting of her historical monuments." This alleged restoration hardly reconciles with the state of deterioration described by Irving when he arrived at the Alhambra less than twenty years later.

The location of Irving's quarters at the Alhambra had much to do with determining the tone and perspective of *The Alhambra*. Irving had occupied the governor's quarters in Charles V's palace for the first weeks of his stay. Prince Dolgorouki remained with him for a few days only in the great cold stone Renaissance building overlooking the court of the cisterns. After Dolgorouki's departure, Irving moved alone on May 29 to an unlikely suite whose rooms today have a plaque above the entrance door recalling his residence.

This door is locked to visitors, but beyond it are four contiguous rooms built by Charles V on the northern embankment wall of the Alhambra. This sixteenth-century addition meant that the fountain garden of Lindaraxa overlooking the embankment and the distant Generalife gardens became an enclosed courtyard. Charles intended the rooms for his personal use during the construction of his palace. Later the suite was refurbished by Philip V for his bride, Elizabeth of Parma.

"The architecture," Irving writes in describing the rooms, "though rich and antiquated, was European. There was nothing Moorish about it. The first two rooms were lofty: the ceilings, broken in many places, were of cedar, deeply panelled and skillfully carved with fruits and flowers, intermingled with grotesque masks or faces." In May 1829, the "ruined apartments" were hardly fit for occupation. The windows "were dismantled and open to wind and weather," the chambers were "desolate," their remote location in the palace "highly dangerous."

To a romantic such details were largely irrelevant. The "doors and windows were soon placed in a state of tolerable security." It was spring. Beyond the fountain courtyard the wondrous palaces were Irving's to wander at will. His vistas included the Generalife gardens, the valley of the Darro and the Gypsy encampments on the farther hills, the adjacent fountain courtyard with its citron and orange trees, and even a view, however oblique, of the interior of the palaces with a distant glimpse of the Court of the Lions. The scent of blossoms filled the air. By moonlight Irving swam alone in the long rectangular pool of the Court of the Myrtles. He sat for hours at his windows "inhaling the sweetness of the garden." It is courting understatement to say that Washington Irving fell in love with the Alhambra.

Today's commemorative plaque above the doorway to these rooms claims that Irving wrote the tales of the Alhambra within. This is largely a flourish aimed at the unremitting flood of tourists passing by daily. Of the forty-one chapters that make up *The Alhambra* Irving may have written two of them here. Like the propagandists of Sintra, Alhambra officials may well have come to believe that the celebrated author actually composed his entire work on the premises. In Irving's case, most of *The Alhambra* was written after his departure (the book appeared three years later); a few tales were even written before he arrived.

During his three-month stay Irving played king of the castle. In one sense, he had earned his right to the throne. In his three years in Spain he had researched, rearranged, translated, and to some degree rewritten Navarrate's biography of Columbus; coupled with that publication he had researched and written *The Conquest of Granada*. He had steeped himself in Arabic and Spanish history. His residency in the Alhambra was a beneficent postgraduate grant.

And now here he was, ensconced in the Alhambra itself, free to stroll about, to explore the labyrinthian complex at will, to savor the moonlight, the flowers, the nightingale's song, the snow-capped vistas of the Sierra Nevadas, the tracery of the stuccoed walls and stalactite ceilings. His refracted vision offered these wonders to him and conveniently blurred the intruding anomalies.

One might well be persuaded, as one is with Dostoyevsky's Florence, that Irving is making a first visit to the Alhambra. But he had been there before. The previous year in fact, when he had spent ten days in Granada, even encountering his guide, Mateo Ximines, on that visit. On March 17, 1828, while within the Alhambra complex, he wrote in his journal: "Hailed by Mateo Ximines from the walls of the Alhambra— later and walk with him among the towers." He visited the Alhambra and the Generalife frequently from his lodgings in Granada, and his journal is filled with unedited enthusiastic jottings.

In *The Alhambra* Irving never claims that his eye is falling freshly upon what he describes. On the other hand he never points out that it is not. He was a successful professional writer and he knew how best to shape his material.

The following year, while living in his suite of rooms at the Alhambra, Irving paid infrequent visits to Granada, where he made social calls and did manuscript research. His royal residence held him a willing captive. He wrote Prince Dolgorouki: "I never had such a delicious abode ... the climate, the air, the serenity and sweetness of the place is almost as seductive as that of the Castle of Indolence." His very ambition was melting to a "mere voluptuousness of sensation." Fortunately for him, Stanley Williams had not yet been born to remind him that life is earnest, life is real, and he should get on with the business of becoming a writer that critics could later extol.

With the exception of his early work, *A History of New*

York and *The Sketch Book of Geoffrey Crayon, Gent., The Alhambra* was Irving's most successful book. In addition to readers attracted to Irving as a teller of tales, *The Alhambra* responded in part to the nineteenth-century infatuation for the Orient, a term used to designate the Islamic Near East, North Africa, and what was then known as the Holy Land. "Orientalism" evoked an exotic, sensual world with unfamiliar terrain, a distinctive culture, and the vividness of light and color. It was exciting. It was sexy. It was vaguely prurient, and in its lack of familiar ethos, enticingly provocative.

The frontispiece of *The Alhambra*'s first edition, published by Carey & Lea in Philadelphia in 1832, reads: "The Alhambra: A series of Tales and Sketches of the Moors and Spaniards, by the Author of the Sketch Book. In two volumes." In the same year the Paris edition published by A. & W. Galignani credits Irving explicitly as the author. Subsequent editions, extensively revised by Irving under his own name, are titled simply *The Alhambra*. The book was ultimately translated into the world's major languages, including the Icelandic (*Soqur fra Alhambra,*) in 1906.

Irving lived in a ruin. He wrote about the Alhambra as if it were at the height of its architectural and esthetic magnificence. Ignoring facts and inventing history, he disarmingly acknowledged that he was creating imaginative romantic legends.

Irving's tales and sketches of *The Alhambra* are written with charm and modesty. His style is honed smooth. He is guaranteed neither to shock nor offend. He entertains his readers generously, with all the gracious overtones of *gentilesse*. He is sometimes tedious in a hostlike way. He knows his subject, and he knows his audience. And best of all, he knows what persona of Washington Irving best suits the narration.

Like *Childe Harold's Pilgrimage*, *The Alhambra* is little read today. But it has a life beyond readership. It moved into that indefinable realm of classics that guarantees permanent recognition. In 1832 it had the power of romantic fascination. It belonged to the travel literature of exotic places at a time when travel was mostly the province of the privileged; it celebrated a history rich both in Orientalism and Spain's Golden Age; and it reminded its readers that miraculously this peerless fortress-palace was still there, waiting for the adventuresome to visit.

Washington Irving himself is little read today. Hailed as America's first writer of distinction, he receives the kind of muted enthusiasm accorded archaic literary figures. In grade schools and college classrooms he is usually encountered in anthologies of American literature. There are few semester-long seminars on Washington Irving.

But the dry, even caustic wit of his early writings brought him the favorable opinion of Byron, who in his correspondence comments admiringly on Irving's writings. No two writers of the romantic period seem less alike in temperament and domestic habits. Irving, the perennial bachelor, exuding social affability, seems asexual. Byron, the rakehell libertine, seems obsessed. But both men shared the power to lure readers to sites they extolled.

Byron and Irving had a close mutual friend in Thomas Moore, the Irish poet, perhaps more famous today for burning Byron's journals than for his own writings. Moore was instrumental in having Irving write his essay on Bryon's ancestral home, Newstead Abbey. Irving arranged to have Moore's life of Byron published by Harpers in the United States.

"One can hardly overstate the influence of the giant romantic upon these two followers of his," writes Williams of Moore's and Irving's relationship to Byron. "[Byron] deeply affected their writings; he had always been to them a subject of admiration and endless speculation." Irving's infatuation with the Alhambra was his most Byronic oblation.

Irving's contemporaries also wrote of the Alhambra. Chateaubriand recounted the loves and tragedies of the Arabs in *The Last of the Abencerrajes* (1826); and both Victor Hugo's *Les Orientales* (1829) and some of Theophile Gautier's work a few years later centered on the Moorish compound. But nothing drew the world's attention to the Alhambra more decisively than Irving's work.

The success of *The Alhambra* both solidified Irving's career and served as a catalyst in changing this "ruinous" site to an international attraction for tourist; some critics say that this result is more ruinous, in terms of falsely conveying a sense of the original palatial compound at its zenith, than if it had been allowed to remain unheralded. For better or worse, Irving's three-month visit to the Alhambra linked his name with the site forever. How the future dealt with it, from crass economic touristic gain to mettlesome scholarly refurbishing, were clearly matters beyond his control.

Today the Alhambra has more than a million visitors a year. The city of Granada, with a population of some 150,000, has over one hundred hotels and pensions. One of these is the Hotel Washington Irving, a turn-of-the-century hostelry. The Irving, as it is known, is located close to the Alhambra, high in the wooded heights. Above the front desk, Irving's portrait smiles beneficently down on the crowded lobby. Here swarms and eddies of tourists from Asia, the Americas, and Europe often create a cacophony of itinerant activity. Irving might well smile. He shares responsibility for their presence.

One-way traffic proceeds from the city up the steep verdant inclines with their swift runnels of sparkling water. At the summit a large parking area accommodates tour buses and cars. A modern administration building stands at the southern end of the Plaza de los Aljibes between the palace of Charles V and the Alcazaba. This building houses a ticket office; a shop selling guidebooks, maps, films, and souvenirs; lavatories, offices; and a room on the second floor reserved for the guides who conduct individuals and groups around the Alhambra. The walls of this room have busts and prints that celebrate both the Alhambra and Mateo Ximines, who served Irving as a guide and a fount of information, some of it spurious but all of it colorful. Mateo Ximines has become the patron saint of the Alhambra guides, who now number about forty or so and all of whom, it is said, are university graduates speaking at least three languages.

The Alhambra is big business. Ticket takers, security personnel, caretakers, gardeners, as well as administrators constitute a formidable payroll. Within the compound today is a post office, several shops, a restaurant, a pension, and a large, elegant government parador converted from the former San Francisco monastery. Unlike Spain's other paradors, there is no mid or low season to observe at this location; rates are permanently pegged at "high season" prices. In January, when the snow filters down from the Sierra Nevada dusting the lions in their famous courtyard, visitors continue unabated. Parador reservations are made half a year in advance.

In 1933, American Ambassador Claude Bowers unveiled a tablet giving Irving's name to the principal avenue running through the Alhambra woods. At the Tower of Justice entrance to the Alhambra, and directly opposite the fountain of Charles V, is a wall plaque of marble reading:

GRANADA

a

WASHINGTON IRVING

1859–1959

Under the plaque is an oval frame that may once have held a likeness of Irving. Below them both is an uninviting fountain trough with an entirely unnecessary admonition not to drink the water. This commemorative tribute, on the hundredth

anniversary of Irving's death, was dedicated by the American
ambassador.

On the reverse side of all admission tickets to the Alhambra is a detailed map of the complex with a route suggested
by red arrows. These arrows pass by a door whose inscription
reads:

WASHINGTON IRVING
escribió en estas habitaciones sus
CUENTOS DE LA ALHAMBRA
en el año 1829

The public is denied admission. But all four of the contiguous rooms are furnished in a style presumably appropriate to
the time of Irving's visit. In the last of these rooms today
stands a polished oak bed in which Irving ostensibly slept.
Carefully made up, the bed has a green brocade bedspread
waiting to be turned down for its occupant's slumber. Were
Irving to awaken in it after a prolonged Rip Van Winkle-like
sleep, he would first see—directly above his head—that the
Italian frescoed ceiling "painted by no mean hand" had
changed from "tolerable preservation" to meticulous restoration. Glancing through his windows, dismantled no longer,
he would see no unruly citron and orange trees able to "fling
their branches into the chamber"; cool green cypresses, senti-
nels of a formal landscape design of boxwood geometrics,
have taken their place.

Rising, he might well suspect that overzealous department-
store interior designers had swept through his rooms on a
frenetic overnight Bloomingdale's-like assignment. His "ruinous" apartment had metamorphosed into a formal suite, a
fashionable decorator's conception of a literary lair. The
walls, once "scrawled over with the insignificant names of
aspiring travelers" are now pristine. The ceilings of the "first
two lofty rooms . . . deep panel work of cedar, richly and

skillfully carved . . . broken in many places" are now entirely whole. The tiled floors, once pitted and chipped, are without imperfection.

A desk stands ready for Irving to write upon (perhaps the ghost of Williams placed it there), a spinnet for him to play, silk embroidered chairs for his guests to sit upon. On the walls hang portraits of Irving as a venerated writer and as a fashionably coiffed young man. Quite matter-of-factly he shares wall space with Ferdinand and his Isabella, the conquerors of the Alhambra.

A mirror above the dressing table reflects a world, as it did for Rip, in which everything is the same and yet transformed. Within the rooms, romantic disarray has become genteel respectability. What had induced a love affair now promotes a platonic alliance. The bedrooms of Proust's Aunt Léonie in Illiers-Combray and of Mark Twain in Connecticut are furnished with the same reverential care. In all three, the one thing that really matters is missing.

Granada's Museo de los Tiros, a sixteenth-century palace now converted into a museum-library, boasts a "Sala de Washington Irving." This room, decorated as the library brochure points out, "with its entirely romantic furnishings is a reminder in all its details of the spirit of foreign travelers, such as Irving . . ." There are portraits and busts of Irving, a picture of Mateo (mysteriously called Matias) Ximines in old age, romantic tints of the Alhamabra, and Irving's profile on Wedgwood china. Elsewhere in the library an entire section is devoted to Irving's works, many of them early editions.

Art historians and critics are at professional odds in determining whether the changes, reconstructions, and restorations of the Alhambra since Irving's time are well advised. Academic and art world disputes are frequently over unacknowledged subtexts, but a man whose viewpoint is never arcane is the Arabic scholar James Dickie, who in 1979 wrote:

Our persistent refusal to interpret the present vestiges
on top of the Alhambra hill in other than a European or
at best a Turkish light accounts for the numerous misconceptions of the Alhambra from the early 19th century, when Europe woke up to the fact of its existence,
down to the present.

Dickie traces some of the changes of the Alhambra since
the defeat of Boabdil in 1492:

Adapted in the Renaissance to lifestyles for which it was
not suited, abandoned as unusable only to be squatted in
by gypsies for 150 years, restored by architects-in-charge
in the 19th and early 20th centuries in accordance with
prevailing Romanticism of the age, and, finally, deliberately maintained today as an ivy-mantled ruin straight
from the pages of Chateaubriand and Washington Irving—
because experimentation has shown that to be the best
way of extracting money from tourists' pockets—by a
Patronato representing the interests of the local *bour-
geoisie,* what confronts us now is but a remnant, the
end-product of an uninterrupted process of metamorpho-
sis over five centuries. It was unfair not to add that it
was the much-derided Romantics who saved the Alhambra. Through the fame their writings conferred on it the
Alhambra became a household word in every modern
language.

If indeed the Romantics saved the Alhambra, Washington
Irving was their commander-in-chief. His "serene and happy
reign," as he himself expressed it, not only made the
Alhambra a household word but enveloped it in the kind of
romantic aura that, however at odds it may be with its
Arabic origins, stubbornly resists effacement. The embodi-

ment of Irving's fantasies and the reality of the present are strikingly akin.

Of the architectural masterpieces left in Spain by the Arabs, including the Mosque at Cordoba and the Alcazar at Seville, the finest today is surely the palaces and gardens of the Alhambra. Their physical location and the artistry of their creation meet in singular esthetic harmony. It is true that the rooms of the Alhambra are empty of furnishings and filled instead with troops of visitors. Without doubt a recognition of the six distinctive palaces, the mosques, and the medina is lost as one moves from room to exquisite room where courtyards and fountains hold one's dazzled attention. But what was once a ruin has become a place of beauty, and beyond its walls the vista of the white houses of Granada in the valley and the distant snow-capped Sierras could stir even the most sated sybarite.

For three months Irving lived in a physically deteriorated Alhambra. Both his literary instincts and his inherent romantic perspective prescribed his view of the Alhambra as he believed it once was. He couldn't help himself. When Irving emerged from his photographer's darkroom, he had turned his stark black-and-white negatives into florid postcards. He had merely to close his eyes a little and allow the refraction to blur. He saw what should have been there and brought it into fictional being. But even he could scarcely have imagined that the future would convert his creative illusion to reality.

6

Mark Twain's Venice

S AMUEL CLEMENS INVENTED MARK TWAIN. HE DRESSED HIM
in a white suit, put a cigar in his mouth, and billowed
his hair into an exuberant mane. He sent Mark Twain
on his first European journey as a travel-journalist. Twain the
iconoclast became an international success. Clemens looked
down upon His work and it was good, even if it took more than
seven days to get Twain in working order. He needed to
make a few adjustments along the way. But when Clemens
got into considerable financial trouble Twain pulled him out
of it.

"The gentle reader will never, never know what a consummate ass he can become until he goes abroad," wrote Twain
in *The Innocents Abroad,* an account of his first trip to
Europe designed to illustrate his observation. "Travel is fatal
to prejudice, bigotry, and narrow-mindedness," he declared,
carefully packing all three.

As a correspondent for the San Francisco *Alta California*
and the New York *Tribune,* Twain sailed on the *Quaker City*
from New York in June 1867, on what was widely advertised
as a "first-class organized tour" of several months. In addi-

tion to being restricted to first-class passengers who paid $1,250 apiece, the tour was the initial such organized cruise from America to Europe. Twain's fare was paid by the *Alta California*. Twain was America's first international tourist. He was thirty-four, on the threshold of a phenomenal career.

He arrived in Venice one month and thirteen days later. His instinctive journalistic response was to engage his readers; his true impression of Venice was another matter. Venice for publication became what he knew others would savor. He embarked on the debunking of the fabled city.

Twain employed one of his most successful journalistic devices by imposing an incongruous middle-American perspective on an exotic foreign setting. What single fact did every American, no matter how untraveled or uneducated, know about Venice? Thus he likened the city to an Arkansas town in flood.

"For a day or two," he wrote of Venice, "the place looked so like an overflowed Arkansas town because of its currentless waters laving the very doorsteps of all the houses, and the cluster of boats made fast under the windows or skimming in and out of the alleys and byways, that I could not get rid of the impression that there was nothing the matter here but a spring freshet, and that the river would fall in a few weeks and leave a dirty-high-water mark on the houses and the streets full of mud and rubbish."

Twain had reached Venice at eight o'clock on a July evening after a "long, long" train ride. In the distance he saw "a great city, with its towers and domes and steeples drowsing in the golden sunset." His unfailing journalistic instinct established his target. Arriving in the city, he set out in a gondola with his companions for the Grand Hotel d'Europe at the junction of the Grand Canal and the Canale della Giudecca.

The storied gondola of Venice!—the fairy boat in which the princely cavaliers of the olden time were wont to cleave the waters of the moonlit canals and look the eloquence of love into the soft eyes of patrician beauties, while the gay gondolier in silken doublet touched his guitar and sang as only gondoliers can sing!

Twain claims that he stepped into a black vehicle that looked like a hearse, "an inky, rusty old canoe with a sable hearse body clapped onto the middle of it." The gay gondolier in silken doublet resembled "a mangy, bare-footed guttersnipe with a portion of his raiment on exhibition which should have been sacred from public scrutiny."

The rusty old canoe "turned a corner" while the gondolier "shot his hearse into a dismal ditch between two long rows of towering, untenanted buildings." Night fell. Lights began to glimmer on the water. The magic of Venice took over. The fairy wand of Twainian romance transformed the canoe into a conveyance that "swept gracefully" into the Grand Canal. Other gondolas passed by "gliding swiftly hither and thither." The gondola advanced "as free and graceful in its gliding movement as a serpent."

The mangy gutternsipe at the controls became a man of "marvelous skill." He turned into a

> picturesque rascal for all he wears no satin harness, no plumed bonnet, no silken tights. His attitude is stately; he is light and supple; all his movements are full of grace. When his long canoe and his fine figure, towering from its high perch on the stern, are cut against the evening sky, they make a picture that is very novel and striking to the foreign eye.

Veteran readers of Twain were not bewildered. They understood that in show business parlance he was working both sides of the house. He aimed to please his readers by covering the full range from burlesque to romance.

His own reaction to Venice is hidden somewhere in the folds of his apparent ambivalence, a Mark Twain characteristic mercilessly explored and analyzed by scholars and critics. He could liken Venice to an aging soubrette, trace the wrinkles and sags, decry the departed grace in the current stumble, be at once ruthless and sentimental, steal descriptive historical material from guidebooks (an invaluable asset for travel writers) while letting a Protestant and midwestern eye fall on Catholic corruption.

Two years after Mark Twain returned from this first European trip he published *The Innocents Abroad*. What one reads today is an extensively edited compilation of some sixty published newspaper articles or "letters," together with material added specifically for the book. He solicited Bret Harte's help in sifting through the articles to cull what seemed worthy and to determine what to embellish. Twain wanted the book to appeal in particular to the eastern establishment. He modified or eliminated some of the subject matter originally slanted for the rougher, less sophisticated westerners.

Twain's portrait of Venice is a classic example of a journalist who deflects his refractive vision in order to elicit maximum readership. This is hardly a federal esthetic offense, but it is different from merely shaping the subject matter to suit the medium. It raises the vexing question of Twain's variation from what physicists call the true angle of deviation.

Twain interwove two themes when discussing the fabled city of canals and carnivals: one is that Venice, once a "haughty, invincible, magnificent republic" has "fallen prey to poverty, neglect, and melancholy decay"; the other is the distinction between the city's romantic nighttime reflection and its daytime reality. The two themes merge to become one overriding motif. The glories of the past are aligned with the allure of the shadowy evening glow; the starkness of the present is linked to sordidness of sunlit clarity.

Twain spent three days and four nights in Venice. At the Grand Hotel d'Europe he wrote four overdue articles about sites recently visited in Italy, and a fifth on Venice. He had little time for sightseeing, but his instinctive professional sense led him immediately to the recognition that he could entertain his readers with the sardonic portrait of a present-day Venice, while instructing them painlessly on a past of some dramatic intensity. Tedious facts did not muddy his rhetorical flow: "This Venice, a haughty, invincible, magnificent republic for nearly fourteen hundred years, whose armies compelled the world's applause whenever and wherever they battled and whose navies well nigh held dominion of the seas." Eleven hundred years is closer to the mark, applause is scarcely the term to describe the reaction of her enemies, and the eastern Mediterranean is something less than "dominion of the seas."

Twain as art critic is, by his own admission, not to be taken seriously ("since one has no opportunity in America to acquire a critical judgment in art") but that scarcely deters him from mocking the "Old Masters." His recognition that Venetian art and religious iconography are inextricably interwoven persuaded him to denounce the source of the subject matter at the expense of the creative artistry. "We have seen pictures of martyrs enough and saints enough to regenerate the world. I ought not to confess it, but still ... it seems that when I have seen one of these martyrs I had seen them all." He senses that Protestant America would relish such remarks: he could attack the art it lacked and the religion it repudiated.

In one sweep he denigrates both the Cathedral of St. Mark and its congregations.

It is built entirely of precious marbles brought over from the Orient ... I could not go into ecstasies over its

coarse mosaics, its unlovely Byzantine architecture . . .
everything was worn out—every block of stone was smooth
and almost shapeless with the polishing hands and shoul-
ders of loungers who devoutly idled here in bygone centuries and have died and gone to the dev—no, simply
died, I mean.

That the Cathedral of St. Mark was an integral part of the
"magnificent" republic he had previous extolled troubled neither Twain nor his readers.

And what of the present? In the Venice of 1867 Twain
sees a city whose piers are deserted, warehouses empty,
merchant fleet vanished, and whose armies and navies
are but memories. "Her glory is departed, and with her
crumbling grandeur of wharves and palaces about her, she
sits among the stagnant lagoons, forlorn and beggared,
forgotten of the world." Ruskin saw this same contemporary
Venice as a city "of graceful arcades and gleaming walls,
veined with azure and warm with gold and fretted with
marble."

From an American materialistic viewpoint, Venice had
suffered the fatal fall from economic grace. Twain writes:
"She that in her palmy days commanded the commerce of a
hemisphere, and made the weal or woe of nations with a
beck of her puissant finger, is become the humblest among
the people of the earth—a peddlar of glass beads for women—
and trifling toys and trinkets for schoolgirls and children."
The decline of an autocrat with puissant finger to a peddlar
with outstretched palm is not one to elicit commiseration
from an American tourist whose nation is bursting with
commerical energy.

But nighttime in contemporary Venice brings shadows casting a delusive glow. "Under the mellow moonlight the Venice of poetry and romance stood revealed . . . clad half in
moon beams and half in mysterious shadows . . . music came

floating over the waters—Venice was complete. It was a beautiful picture—very soft and dreamy beautiful."

At night, as well, during a grand fete, "all Venice was abroad on the water, rockets splendidly illuminated all the gondolas ... colored lamps hung aloft ... lighting up the faces of the young and the sweetscented and lovely below." Twain calls the scene enchantingly beautiful.

> Under the charitable moon her stained palaces are white again, their battered sculptures are hidden in shadows, and the old city seemed crowned once more with the grandeur that was hers five hundred years ago. In the moonlight her fourteen centuries of greatness fling their glories about her, and once more is she the princeliest among the nations of the earth.

Daybreak strips Twain's Venice of artifice. ". . . In the glare of day there is little poetry about Venice ... in the treacherous sunlight we see Venice decayed, forlorn, poverty-stricken, and commerceless—forgotten and utterly insignificant." Far from forgotten, the fame of Venice was constant, the reason in fact for Twain's presence there. Travelers sought out the city for esthetic and less elevated reasons, and some of these visitors, like Byron, confirmed its reputation as an exotic site.

One of those "stained palaces" that the moon rendered white had belonged to Byron, who lived in Venice some fifty years before Twain's brief visit. The Venetian Byron bore little resemblance to the relatively obscure and entirely untraveled young romantic whom we met in Sintra. Byron had become a major celebrity, his role as rake vying with that as poet. He lived first in comparative poverty in Venice, then, on the assumption of his heritage, he raised the kind of scandalous hell that sustained his notoriety. His palace on the Grand Canal, his amorous exploits, his social and political involvements all served to link his name with Venice perhaps more than any other city in his lifetime. Here he met the Countess Grigioli, who became his last mistress.

Byron took the city as he found it; her illustrious past gifted him with a metropolis of radiant beauty and esthetic distinction; her morality was no better than it should be and he did nothing to elevate the tone. The church was something of a colorful scandal, but then so was he. The beggars who so offended Mark Twain were for Byron an inevitable part of any social fabric. Byron's genuine concern for the common man and for his freedom never interfered with his unspoken aristocratic awareness that without the visible contrast of plebian poverty, wealth and rank would lose more than a modicum of its powerful attraction. Twain visited Venice as an "innocent" tourist, using the city to serve his journalistic needs; Byron lived in Venice as a sophisticated, some would say decadent, resident.

Twain falls on the Catholic Church in Venice—and elsewhere in Italy—with the sting of a wasp. He withholds no negative observation, confident that both his editors and his readers shared his Protestant prejudices. The wealth of the church, in a city that abounds in poverty, offends him. He dislikes the preponderance of clergy, the explicit iconography, the immensity of cathedrals, and he especially hates the clusters of beggars who gather around the church doors asking for alms. Twain sees mendicancy as the direct economic product of Catholicism.

"In Venice," Twain writes, "today a city of a hundred thousand inhabitants, there are twelve hundred priests." On the stoops of churches he discovers that "wretchedness and poverty abound . . . many heads were humbly bowed, and as many hands extended, appealing for pennies—appealing with foreign words we could not understand, but appealing mutely, with sad eyes and sunken cheeks, and ragged raiment that no words were needed to translate."

The contrast when one enters the church is stunning: "Then we passed within the great doors, and it seemed that the riches of the world were before us.... As far as I can see, Italy for fifteen hundred years has turned all her energies, all her finances, and all her industry to the building up of a vast army of wonderful church edifices, and starving half her citizens to accomplish it. She is today one vast museum of magnificence and misery."

Travel may be fatal to prejudice, bigotry, and narrow-mindedness, as Twain maintained, but here all thrive in his journalistic persona. Italy's contributions "for fifteen hundred years" to the worlds of literature, science, art, and architecture (with which he knew better than to burden his readers) are ignored by Twain as he obsessively concentrates on the social and cultural defects of religion. "All the churches in an ordinary American city put together could hardly buy the jewelled frippery in one of her hundred cathedrals, and for every beggar in America, Italy can show a hundred—and rags and vermin to match. It is the wretchedest, princeliest land on earth."

Twain's view of the church was reinforced when he went to the Duomo in Florence, immediately following his three days in Venice. He sees the edifice under Brunelleschi's dome as

a vast pile that has been sapping the purses of her citizens for five hundred years, and it is not nearly finished yet. Like all other men, I fell down and worshipped it, but when the filthy beggars swarmed around me the contrast was too striking, too suggestive, and I said, "O sons of classic Italy, *is* the spirit of enterprise, of self-reliance, of noble endeavor, utterly dead within ye? Curse your indolent worthlessness, why don't you rob your church?"

It was Twain who pointed out that only by going abroad can one know what a consummate ass one can become. This call to Emersonian self-reliance and Thoreauvian independence, to say nothing of anarchy, is wonderfully amusing as he well knew. "Three hundred happy, comfortable priests are employed in that cathedral," Twain concludes. Few writers knew better than Twain how to shape their prose to fit their thematic needs, but in the matter of Italy's church he seems to have lost a fair measure of balance.

Fortunately for the reader, this allowed him further bombast of the absurd at which he excelled. He describes the frescoes in the tombs of the Medici family as depicting "their trivial, forgotten exploits on land and sea . . . with the Savior and the Virgin throwing bouquets to them out of the clouds, and the Diety himself applauding from his throne in heaven!"

As a title, *The Innocents Abroad* suggests that American travelers brought to foreign lands a freshness of perception undimmed by corrupt worldliness. The title richly rewards the assumption that the book will offer numerous incidents where innocence is amusingly confronted by experience. Twain understood the fine line between innocence and ignorance, but *The Ignorants Abroad* was hardly likely to encourage enthusiastic book sales from his traveling companions. Not all the *Quaker City* tour group were ignorant about the sites they were visiting. Many "read up" on the countries and places they were to visit and they often arrived at locations in pre-exam readiness for what awaited them. But if prejudice is one of the hallmarks of ignorance, the bias against Catholicism on the part of the American Protestant innocents abroad in Twain's time stemmed more from ignorance than from analysis of the role of the Catholic Church during the Middle Ages and the Renaissance in Europe.

In his chapters on Venice Twain satirizes the pretensions of the American innocent. He lists Italian hotel registrations, supposedly copied verbatim, in which the American registrants, after a brief sojourn in France, seem compelled while in Italy to list themselves as coming from "*Amerique,*" sometimes accompanied by "*trois amis.*" "It is not pleasant to see an American thrusting his nationality forward obtrusively in a foreign land, but oh, it is pitiable to see him making of himself a thing that is neither male nor female, neither fish, flesh, nor fowl—a poor, miserable, hermaphrodite Frenchman!"

In Venice Twain came upon a curious phenomenon, a black guide from South Carolina whose parents had brought him to Venice as an infant. He spoke four languages. He "is a worshiper of art and thoroughly conversant with it; knows the history of Venice by heart and never tires of talking of her illustrious career. He dresses better than any of us, I think, and is daintily polite." This "cultivated Negro, the offspring of a South Carolina slave" was said by Twain to be the only guide "we have had yet who knew anything." Negroes, Twain wrote, "are deemed as good as white people in Venice, and so this man feels no desire to go back to his native land. His judgment is correct." *Adventures of Huckleberry Finn* was still almost twenty years away.

Venice inevitably calls to mind Twain's personal and professional connection with water as a means of travel and escape. The canals of Venice are a long way from the Mississippi, and the hearselike gondola scarcely resembles Huck's raft, but water is water, and whether it is a paddle-wheel steamer, or a gondola, or a canoe, the conveyance must float to its destination. In his *Alta California* article on Venice, Twain used some seven hundred words to describe his first gondola ride. When assembling material for *The Innocents Abroad* he correctly surmised that the most exotic aspect of Venice to "the foreign eye" was its canals and the gondolas that plied them. He added thirteen hundred words to the original seven hundred on the gondola.

Twain is solidly in the tradition of American writers whose

refraction of the European scene emphasizes contrast with American life. These distinctions, as Washington Irving was the first to show, sharpen both images. Irving viewed the Alhambra, and Spain itself for that matter, in a rather mellow light, but his republicanism brought an uncommon perspective to the European setting. He left at home much of Twain's triad of bigotry, narrow-mindedness, and prejudice. But Twain used this first journalistic European assignment as a way of being entertainingly critical of the strangeness he encountered. Strangeness meant different from America. He made his fellow travelers, and indeed himself, the butt of many of his observations. Twain was a tourist, Irving a traveler. Stripped of his bias, Twain as he well knew was in danger of rendering his prose bland and unengaging.

Nineteenth-century American writers in general wrote about Europe in the "you-can't-go-home-again" vein. The analogy of Europe as cultural birthplace and home, and America as contemporary residence underlay much of such writing. But Twain attempted what no other American writer had done: to contrast the European scene with uncompromising Yankee, midwestern, and far-western images. In his role as skeptic, determined not to be hoodwinked, bamboozled, or hornswoggled, he advanced views so outrageous that their absurdity becomes the issue. His rhetorical instinct led him unerringly to convert scenes to homespun Americana. Venetian palaces became semi-detached houses with doorsteps, gondolas became canoes, canals became alleys and byways. His readers loved such analogies. They made him America's leading humorist.

With *The Innocents Abroad* Twain became the first tourist writer. His place in the hierarchy of American writers seeking identity in Europe is secure. He wrote the initial book on touring. He was a tourist in the sense that we understand the term today. The *Quaker City* advertised herself as "the first organized pleasure party ever assembled for a transat-

lantic voyage." Places to be visited were determined before-
hand, reservations and travel arrangements undertaken by
the organizers, who accepted responsibility and profit alike.

Like many tourists, Twain seems not to have objected that
the sense of individual travel discovery was replaced by the
convenience of being escorted to places already determined
by others as worthy of a visit. Bret Harte (with whom Twain
had a later falling out) observed: "Yet, for all his independence, 'Mark Twain' seems to have followed his guide and
guidebooks with a simple, unconscious fidelity. He was quite
content to see only that which everybody else sees, even if he
was not content to see it with the same eyes . . ."

But to a large extent he *did* see it with the same eyes, as a
middle-class WASP with a deep suspicion of High Art and
High Church. But he described what he saw with such a
fresh voice, such an uninhibited enthusiasm for detailing the
idiosyncratic aspects of the experience itself that he established a genre that has generated periodicals, newspaper
travel sections, and a belief on the part of tourists themselves
(as was true of his fellow passengers on the *Quaker City,*
most of whom set out furiously writing travel journals whose
inspiration diminished in proportion to the time consumed
by the journey) that their individual travel experiences are
not only bound to be of interest to others but that they have
the talent to write professionally about them.

Twain knew that the best way to counter critical objection
to *The Innocents Abroad* was to make few claims for the
value of the work, thereby encouraging the reader to contra-
dict him. He was not writing "a record of a solemn scientific
expedition . . . it was only a record of a picnic" and if it had
any virute it was to suggest to the reader that this "was how
he would be likely to see Europe." Readers seemed immune
to condescension.

Mark Twain wanted to see more of Venice. He came back.
This "deranged . . . utterly insignificant" city was ripe for

journalistic exploitation. Twain returned to Venice in 1878 and 1892, on both occasions accompanied by his wife, Mrs. Samuel Clemens (Mrs. Mark Twain did not exist). Beneath the surface of Twain's professional lure for Venice appears to be a strong personal attachment to the city that caused him to buy an extravagantly carved bed in October 1878. He and Mrs. Clemens had it shipped to America to be placed in the master bedroom of the Clemenses' large new house in Hartford, Connecticut. The bed became an integral part of their private and personal life.

It is tempting to succumb to facile analysis and suggest that the Mark Twain who returned to Venice to satirize the city further in *Roughing It* was he who first saw it in the treacherous daylight; that the romantic Venice seen by moonlight prompted Samuel Clemens to bring his wife and children there. In that latter spirit the carved bed was purchased, to become the matrimonial bed "with space enough for a family"; but after Olivia Langdon Clemens died, the bed shifted owners from Samuel Clemens to become the domain of Mark Twain. It became, indeed, a publicity platform, photographed and written about, a four-poster office in which Twain spent his mornings dictating and writing.

This bed, now on display in the master bedroom on the second floor of the Mark Twain Memorial in Hartford, Connecticut, may well offer the final word on Mark Twain and Venice. Or, perhaps more modestly, one might say a final comment. He paid two hundred dollars for it. Carved of black walnut, the bed is six feet long and about five and a half feet wide. The bedposts are convoluted spirals on top of which are busts of winged cherubs. The headboard is an inverted V, whose sides support cupids in a jagged frieze, their arms raised to hold garlands they appear to be weaving in and out of a heavy loop of drapery. It is hard to find an unadorned inch on the footboard, with its intricate scroll and acanthus carving, surmounted by a sunburst cherubim looking down upon a relief of recumbent children.

The football-size angels atop the bedposts unscrew from the columns and are said to have been playthings of the Twain children when they were ill. Playing with cupids from the bedposts of one's parents' matrimonial bed is the kind of heritage that keeps analysts solvent.

Although the bed is now back in the Hartford house, its first American resting place, it moved about even as Twain did, first to his New York City apartments on both Fifth Avenue and West 10th Street, and later to Stormfield, Twain's house in Redding, Connecticut, where he spent the last years of his life.

Twain looked upon the bed as "this . . . old elaborately carved black Venetian bedstead—the most comfortable bedstead that ever was, and with space enough in it for a family, and carved angels enough surmounting its twisted columns and its headboard and footboard to bring peace to the sleepers, and pleasant dreams."

Twain is said to have been the most famous man in the world at the time of his death in 1910. His popularity as a writer was fanned and augmented by his relentless self-promotion and his worldwide travels until his face and figure had global recognition. The Venetian bed became public domain. Depending on one's viewpoint, it could be seen either as a stage setting or a throne. Twain was photographed in this bed on numerous occasions (the *New York Times* printed a shot of him propped up with many pillows in the Venetian bed in the spring of 1906). He gave interviews from its depths, he received visitors while he was ensconced in the bed, he dictated his autobiography from the bed, which soon took on a role of its own as a kind of supine office space. His daughter commented that "the bed habit is the recipe for father's success." Twain's bed became as much of a *mise-en-scène* as did the bed of Proust's Aunt Léonie with her apothecary-altar bedtable.

Twain's bed today is roped off to preserve it from the inquisitive hands of tour groups marching through the rooms in the Hartford Memorial. On the bedstand next to the bed is a gas lamp (said to have worked sporadically and even dangerously in Twain's time), books, a large ashtray to catch the ever-falling cigar ashes, a notebook waiting for the master to fill it. Only the equivalent of Aunt Léonie's madeleine is missing.

The bed is made up with pillows at the footboard. Mark Twain slept with his head here, the better to admire the sculpted Venetian headboard. The general impression of the bed is one of such massive inappropriateness in a room with its plain wooden doors and New England furniture that it is something of a delightful eccentric joke. The extravagance of Venice could hardly come to rest in a less likely spot.

Several years ago the curators of Hartford's Mark Twain Memorial had the bed (and other furniture) refurbished and restored. It developed that the posts of the bed date to the seventeenth century. The headboard, footboard, and siderails are all of the nineteenth century. The famous bed, like its owner, was a composite.

But the bed reflects amusingly on Twain's response to Venice. It calls for an occupant whose sense of what he wants last to see before he dozes off is the antithesis of decorative simplicity, an occupant who chooses to be reminded of Venice not only at night, but during the day when, as he wrote, he would remain in it "dictating ... morning after morning, with so much serenity."

Altogether too easily the bed comments on the ambivalence between Twain's advocacy of an unaffected view of life and Clemens's attraction to the fanciful, on the link between Twain's public performances and Clemens's private preferences. In the end it is merely a piece of furniture, nothing more than a massive black walnut carved bed bought in Venice. But both Twain and Clemens shipped it several thousand miles to lie in it, and, ultimately, to die in it.

7

Cervantes' La Mancha

U NLIKE HOMER AND CHAUCER WITH THEIR MYTHIC CITADEL-
bastion, Proust with his revisionary childhood domain,
Byron and Irving with their romanticized sites, or
Dostoyevsky and Twain with their cities of disenchantment,
Cervantes' La Mancha seems to have passed through the
crystalline prism of his imagination to emerge virtually unaltered in its guise as the fictional world of his epic novel.

The landscape created by Cervantes for *Don Quixote* had two
dimensions: the surface La Mancha serves all save his protagonist; while La Mancha as a mirage—haunting, evocative, filled
with theatrical illusion—accommodates Don Quixote alone.

Some four hundred years have passed since the publication
of *Don Quixote*. Apart from the Bible, *Don Quixote* is said to
be the world's most translated book. In 1605, Cervantes
chose La Mancha, this high tableland of seemingly infinite
Spanish horizons covering some 18,260 square miles, as the
setting of his novel. La Mancha includes much of four Spanish provinces (Ciudad Real, Albacete, Toledo, and Cuenca) in
the heart of the Iberian peninsula.

La Mancha is mostly flat. Sparsely populated with few

cities among the widely separated towns and villages, La Mancha has Roman-straight roads on which you can travel unencountered for miles. It is a region of tradition and legend and superstition; a place of hard manual labor on farms and vineyards. Winter is cold and biting; autumn dank and windswept. Summer is often scalding. In spring La Mancha has breathtaking beauty: flowering pink-and-white apple and cherry trees, scarlet poppies lining the roadside, purple saffron in undulating waves, fields of yellow and blue wildflowers.

As they did in Cervantes' time, the castles continue to mount guard, their crenelated battlements as romantic and redundant as they were then; the whitewashed windmills still line the hillocks, silhouetted against the translucent skyline; the seignorial mansions stand almost unaltered in the towns, their portals etched with noble escutcheons.

Spain reveres Cervantes. He is celebrated as the country's world-renowned literary figure, the peer of Shakespeare (they died on the same day, give or take a different-calendar week). For Spaniards, Cervantes represent all that is dark-toned and brilliant in their national ethos. Their laughter is at the heart of his fiction, as is their hard-won cynicism. Universities extol him; elementary-school primers begin with him; his name is given to countless streets and parks and institutes and commercial establishments; his likeness, progressively more dashing and handsome as the passage of years since his demise lengthens, is found in art galleries, in museums, on public statues, busts, stamps, currency, and cigar bands. Madrid, Seville, Toledo, and indeed every city or town in which he spent time (in prison and out) claims him as a native son. And if his literary fame were not enough, every schoolchild knows that he lost the use of his left arm in Spain's glorious victory over the Turks and their infidel allies at the sea battle of Lepanto.

La Mancha, however, reveres not Cervantes but his characters. La Mancha sees itself forever immortalized as the home of Quixote and Sancho. Here Cervantes is upstaged by his own creations. His two fictional characters stepped out of his imagination into their own world with as much independent existence as their immediate contemporaries, Hamlet and Lear, who are no more universal and God knows, as the Spanish point out, not nearly so amusing.

Dostoyevsky when living in Florence wrote to his niece on the "boundless" problem of portraying a "positively" good man: ". . . of the good figures in Christian literature, the most complete is that of Don Quixote. But he is good only because at the same time he is ridiculous . . . compassion for the good man who is ridiculed and who is unaware of his own worth generates sympathy in the reader. And this ability to arouse compassion is the very secret of humor." That compassion and humor, prototypically Spanish, account for La Mancha's deification of Quixote and Panza.

Pictorial likenesses of the knight and the squire are at the entrance of every town in La Mancha. Their names are given to restaurants, roadside stands, taverns, cafés, bars, canteens, and gas stations. One finds them on menus, matchboxes, T-shirts, and tawdry touristic souvenirs by the hundred. But to an uncommon degree, the spirit of Quixote and Rocinante, his skinny nag, and Sancho with Dapple, his obdurate donkey, transcends commerce.

Those who live in La Mancha's towns and farms and vineyards think of themselves as direct descendants of the novel's characters. Whether in truth the dwellers on La Mancha's plains have remained as unchanged as their landscapes is at best a moot point. It may well be that the salient characteristics of Cervantes' fictional men and women are supremely human rather than individually distinctive, in which case the men and women we encounter in La Mancha today are not so much unchanged as they are testaments to Cervantes' novelistic art. And every so often one has a fleeting sense that the Manchegans are behaving in a Cervantine manner as an unconscious imitative tribute to the novel rather than instinctively.

The landscape of La Mancha reveals much about Cervantes' creative imagination, but readers of *Don Quixote* who go there to trace the route of the knight of the rueful countenance and his squire travel (as I soon discovered) in vain. No such route exists. Cervantes deliberately eschewed specificity. He vacillated. He kept most of his locations vague, recognizable only in the most general terms. He became the cartographer of a map on which precise detail is irrelevant and illusory inexplicitness deliberate.

None of this has prevented scholars and students and dilettantes, enthusiastic readers and cranks from setting out to discover the route. They even have real maps to follow, one of them made for the 1780 edition of *Don Quixote* under the patronage of Spain's Royal Academy and inscribed: "Map of Spain that recognizes the places visited by Don Quixote and the locations of his adventures." These locations were "delineated" by Don Joseph de Hermosilla, Captain of Engineering. The map succeeds in being both difficult to read and wildly improbable.

In a series of lectures on the novel at Harvard in 1951–52, Vladimir Nabokov chose *Don Quixote* as the logical starting point to discuss the development of the genre. Although Nabokov is generally scornful of critics who lack a knowledge of their author's language (viz. his book on Gogol, in which he claims that a "great literary achievement is a phenomenon of language and not one of ideas"), he relied on a translation by Samuel Putnam of Cervantes' sixteenth-century Spanish.

Nabokov drew a map of Spain on the blackboard, wrote "Old Castile" at its center, and in smaller letters, "La Mancha." He pinpointed the towns of El Toboso, the home of Dulcinea, and Argamasilla, the starting point of the adventures. Nabokov claimed that Cervantes seemed to know Spain as little as Gogol did central Russia.

"If," Nabokov told his students,

> we examine Don Quixote's excursions topographically we are confronted by a ghastly muddle . . . throughout these adventures there is a mass of monstrous inaccuracies at every stop. The author avoids descriptions that would be particular and might be verified. It is quite impossible to follow these rambles in Central Spain across four or six provinces . . . Cervantes's ignorance of places is wholesale and absolute, even in respect of Argamasilla in the La Mancha district, which some consider more or less the starting point.

Either Nabokov's students grasped that Cervantes' wholesale and absolute ignorance of places stemmed from his intimate familiarity with such locations, or they should have been pumping gas in Chiliwaukee, Iowa, not attending Nabokov's class at Harvard.

Not long ago I set out on a quest to see how the spirit of Don Quixote and Sancho Panza pervaded La Mancha. My own journey to trace Cervantes' uncharted course seemed at least no more focused than the one he gave Quixote, and I was aware that the comparison didn't end there.

I decided to visit three towns specifically mentioned in the novel: Argamasilla de Alba, the ostensible starting point, Puerto Lapice, a likely location for the inn at which Quixote was dubbed knight, and El Toboso, the home of the peerless Dulcinea. On my journey I expected to encounter windmills and castles, ancient inns and remote villages. I had no idea that I would come upon a Renaissance town, Almagro, with an active open-pit theater that had presented Cervantes' plays during his lifetime. Even less did I expect to find in a remote, godforsaken little La Mancha town a sixteenth-century Italian

Renaissance palace, in mint condition, built by Cervantes' commander-in-chief at Lepanto, the Marquis de Santa Cruz.

I first sought out Argamasilla de Alba, population 6,537, a town so insignificant that it is not even on Spain's official roadmap. Some scholars believe that this was the hometown of Don Quixote and Sancho Panza, and the place as well where Cervantes himself lived while writing the early part of the novel. To the citizens of Argamasilla these are facts, not speculations. Cervantes says merely that his protagonist lived in "a village of La Mancha whose name I do not wish to remember," which is rather different from not being able to remember. Three epitaphs and three sonnets, all of them of deliberately dubious quality, are ascribed at the end of part I of the novel to academicians of "Argamasilla, a village of La Mancha."

At the outskirts of Argamasilla is a white brick wall. On it is a profile in black of Quixote and Rocinante, the name of the town, and the inscription taken from the novel, "A village of La Mancha" (literally "A place of La Mancha"). Tourist brochures say that "the spirit of Don Quixote still lives in Argamasilla," and that "the living presence of the knight . . . gives the village its charm for the visitor." Not for this visitor. Charm is a quality I found singularly lacking in Argamasilla. "The living presence of the knight," despite a diligent search, eluded me.

In Argamasilla is the Cave of Medrano, a secluded cellar that Cervantes reputedly used as a study. To find it, I drove over unpaved back streets of the town, navigating some of the most formidable potholes in La Mancha. I asked directions of five persons, each time drawing nearer to what was known to everyone as a "green door" behind which was said to be the possessor of the key to the Cave of Medrano.

The key holder turned out to be an old woman, bent practically double, who took me across the street to a barnlike structure that contained an inner patio. Here she sat down, sighed heavily, extracted a token entrance fee, pointed to a whitewashed cellar entrance, placed her trembling hand at the ready on an electric switch so that not a moment of illumination would be wasted, and told me to go ahead on my own.

The Cave of Medrano revealed itself as a warren of underground rooms spectrally lighted (I reflected uneasily that the old woman could cast me at will into everlasting darkness) and furnished in someone's idea of an appropriate location to write a classic work of literature, reminding me irresistibly of the designer of Irving's rooms at the Alhambra. But here the interior was spartan: a table, a stool, a candle, a woven mat on the wall over a couch of stone, a sword and a lance used as decorative wall hangings.

Proceeding reluctantly to further inner rooms—ambition pushed me on, exhorting me to research heights, while I cravenly longed to retreat to daylight—I came upon a rogue's gallery of shoulder-high busts of all the characters in the novel. All of them. In deference to the spirit that initiated this memorial location I will not comment on the quality of the artwork or the absurdity of the conception.

I rejoined the old woman, none too soon for my tastes. She tried to sell me a book on the history of Argamasilla de Alba, about which I knew too much already, and some postcards that I was happy to purchase. I tipped her generously, not least because she honored her light-switch stewardship.

The next town I sought out was Puerto Lapice on National Highway IV, the direct route between Madrid and the south of Spain. Thousands upon thousands of cars and trucks pass through Puerto Lapice every year. Puerto Lapice was born to be a way-stop, and it is here supposedly that Don Quixote was knighted by the obliging innkeeper. Today, a large commerical establishment calling itself "Don Quixote's Inn" serves travelers, truckers, and busloads of tour groups. Tables are set out in a courtyard; nearby is an active souvenir stand. On the menu, extensive enough to satisfy a trencher, one finds listed good local wines from neighboring Valdepenas.

The inn is whitewashed, with accents of blinding blue. The tone of the establishment is resolutely commerical and somewhat ironic: no one believes that this really was the inn chosen by Cervantes for Don Quixote's most significant chivalric ceremony, but on the other hand, given that four hundred years have passed, it is at least in the approximate geographic location.

The inn does a big business—it is about one hundred miles south of Madrid, just the right distance to warrant indulgence in one of those leisurely two-or-three-hour repasts that are in themselves more timelessly Cervantine than any vaunted location. Puerto Lapice is a busy town; you have to look both ways before crossing the main street. It is the kind of place that satisfies your material needs and never for a moment persuades you to consider a return visit.

By now I was beginning to get the idea: not specific locations but metaphysical occurrences concerned Cervantes. Nevertheless I knew that I must visit one town that he mentions repeatedly. This was El Toboso, the home of the peerless Dulcinea, a woman whose like never existed. Dulcinea, incomparably beautiful and irrefutably virtuous, lived in what Quixote called "the great city of Toboso."

El Toboso was a parched little village in the seventeenth century and it remains a parched little village now. Don Quixote's fantasy about an ideal woman was matched by Cervantes' choice of El Toboso as the place for her to dwell. Readers unfamiliar with the arid region of La Mancha, then and now, might even imagine that El Toboso was one of those enchanting whitewashed Spanish towns, all red-tiled roofs and black-grilled balconies.

El Toboso is nothing of the sort. A visit persuades one of the irony of Cervantes' choice. Except for the main thoroughfare, most of El Toboso's streets are unpaved, and the wind coming across the vast plains of La Mancha whips up eddies of dust at every corner. A brave sign at the entrance of the town directs the visitor to the "urban center" where the stoops facing the streets are swept and washed down every day.

El Toboso's being something of an international joke is not altogether resented by those who live there. They know that the joke will attract a modest stream of visitors, and despite their poverty they have made honorable provisions accordingly. In the town hall, a concierge will take you to a nearby "library" that contains thirty-four different editions in a variety of languages. Many of these are signed by past and current heads of state, some of whom, one is reasonably certain, have only a scantling familiarity with the novel's thousand pages.

In the town square is a witty sculpture of the knight, who lends himself to that sort of thing, and another of the flawless Dulcinea, who does not. The town hall provides a little map for following the route that Don Quixote and Sancho Panza took when they arrived in El Toboso (in chapter 9 of part II of the novel). It offers a fine look at the town's austere houses, some of them as old as the novel itself. And one can visit, at prescribed hours, and never on Monday, Dulcinea's house.

This reputed residence of a fictional character was once the dwelling place of a wealthy female landowner, and while it has been much altered and renovated since the seventeenth century, it does give one a sense of how the gentry in a small village may have lived. The civic employee that takes one around is loyal to the tradition that this was the house of Dulcinea. She speaks as if Dulcinea had lived there. We enter Dulcinea's bedroom, note the handwoven bedspread, the embroidered pillowcase, and the geranium on the windowsill. We know immediately that it belongs in the pantheon of the bedchamber of Proust's Aunt Léonie, the

Alhambra suite of Washington Irving, and the "memorial" home of Mark Twain with his Venetian bed.

El Toboso has accepted its role as the butt of Cervantes' ironic treatment with exceptional dignity and good grace. It may not be a "great city," but it is not a village to take lightly. El Toboso emerges as an authentic site in any search for the novel's locales.

My quest came to seem not so much foolish as misdirected. A novel about reality and shifting illusion doesn't lend itself to investigations centering on the former at the expense of the latter. La Mancha itself, that extensive, eerie, and strikingly level tableland, that landscape of straight lines, combines both geometric form and imaginative content, exacting detail and visual deception.

Rows of olive trees, perfectly aligned, vie with files of grape vines to touch the horizon. The roads themselves extend for miles with neither curve nor incline. The towns have narrow streets intersecting one another with a gridlike precision. Uniform fences outline undeviating boundaries of property; highway crossings are meetings of asphalt strips that lead to infinity.

Yet hovering over this diagrammic grid is a mirage. Cervantes knew precisely what he was about when he chose La Mancha for Quixote's peregrinations. The heat of summer (when Quixote set out) and the absence of rainfall promote clouds of dust. Sometimes such clouds rise from the descendants of the novel's "flocks of ewes and rams," but more often today they are caused by farm vehicles; they could just as well come, as Quixote imagined, from an army of soldiers marching on a course of invasion.

Once the heat of the day sets in, La Mancha's plains burn under a merciless sun. Shimmering vapors impede clarity of vision. Quixote adventured in a land whose illusory properties reflected his mental and emotional state.

Windmills—surely the most famous of Quixote's conceits

and one that symbolizes endeavors as futile as my own foot- ling search for his ethereal spirit—are sometimes marshaled in Manchegan rows along distant hilltops. When their arms are whirling they look like creatures in states of frenzied animation. They may not resemble giants but they indubit- ably have lives of their own. Significantly, many persons today envision them primarily in terms of the knight's misconception.

At night—and La Mancha is no exception to night sounds that lend themselves to frightening interpretation—in the darkness of Manchegan groves, winds roar through the trees and join with "terrifying" and unidentifiable noises. Owls call to one another. Trains whistle. A rush of wings is fol- lowed by the distant cry of some small creature in distress. But Cervantes had no need to stress the illusions of night- time—as territory for Quixote's fancies it was too easily achieved.

Perhaps the castles of La Mancha evoke the chivalric hal- lucinations of Don Quixote better than anything else. Such castles, both Moorish alcazars and Spanish fortresses, dot this area which for centuries served as a battleground for the Moorish-Spanish conflict. By the time Don Quixote rode out in the first decade of the seventeenth century, almost four centuries to the year had passed since the famous Knights of Calatrava had conclusively defeated the Arabs in La Mancha in 1212. Ancient maps refer to La Mancha as the *Campo de Calatrava*.

Many of the La Mancha castles, in their state of ruinous decay, ironically look more romantic to us today than they would if they were in mint condition. Perhaps the most dramatic ruin is the 1217 castle-fortress of the Knights of Calatrava atop a strategic hillside near the village of Calzada de Calatrava. This location is on the southern border of La Mancha; beyond it lie the Sierra Morena, the peaks of Andalusia, and the Mediterranean. The Moors had Andalusian strongholds until their final defeat in Granada in 1492.

This Calatrava castle is approached by a single track that winds upward over a rocky surface. The arched entranceway is cut into a wall of stones. The castle has lost none of its fearsome sense of purpose. Inside it is dark and intimidating. A caretaker who lives in the windswept lonely spot will take you around and unlock the chapel door; inside, much restored, one finds brick vaulting ascribed to Moslem prisoners. Above the west door is the cusped stonework of a rose window.

The castle-fortress has three stout perimeters, the second built into the rock; *massive* is the word that comes to mind when standing on the ramparts. To the northeast, the plains of La Mancha stretch to the line of the horizon; but immediately to the south and west are the foothills of the Sierra Morena, the range that separates La Mancha from a culturally and topographically distinctive southern Spain—from this uncompromising and demanding terrain to an area of flowers, sunshine, and the sparkling sea.

The fortress thus serves as an observation point for both the mountain passes and the tableland. Well before the time of the impressionable Don Quixote, from these towers one could see the ruins of the Salvatierra Castle, where in 1158 the Abbot of Fiero founded the Order of Calatrava, the first of Spain's military orders. This castle was captured by the Moslems and held until 1212 when the victorious Calatrava knights began building their own fortress-castle.

Almost one hundred miles due north is another La Mancha castle to inspire Cervantes' knight errant. On a promontory outside the town of Consuerga, this edifice was once a stronghold of the Spanish branch of the Knight's Hospitallers of the Order of Saint John of Jerusalem. It comes dangerously close to being a parody of turreted chivalric might.

Rising directly out of a rough-hewn rock summit, the castle's exterior consists almost entirely of three-quarter-faced contiguous towers; narrow slits in these towers serve as lookout windows and attack stations; to one side are crenelated battlements; the towers have turrets with merlons and corbels; the entranceway, up a wide flight of steps, leads to a portcullis gateway, and beyond that a massive studded door reinforced with iron grating.

Next to the castle, extending to the limit of the rocky promontory, is a line of white windmills. In the bright sunlight, the windmills and the castle in this deserted spot seem today too picturesque to be taken seriously. But it is strangely inhospitable: the winds up here are bitter cold even in late March, and in the summertime it is hotter than the scorching plains. The castle proper does not admit visitors, and even the most determined adventurer could not scale the walls.

Cervantes, looking about him in La Mancha, saw these castles and windmills; his protagonist made them part of his life. We are the heirs of romanticism, Cervantes its percursor by two centuries. We look at the world differently. We see the crenelated battlements, the turrets, keeps, casement windows, portcullis entranceways, huge studded doors, parapets, ramparts, and towers through eyes misted by the romantic age, our antecedent by another two centuries. Don Quixote of La Mancha saw them as the logical and appropriate local *mise-en-scène* for defenders of chivalry such as he imagined himself to be.

Chivalric knights were the servants of God. Warring Spaniards saw the Moors as the enemy, first of all, of the Christian God. The churches of La Mancha have paintings and images that celebrate the miracles that form the imaginative rather than the conceptual basis of Christianity. A miracle is reality transformed. Don Quixote's interweaving of illusion and reality had a solid religious background. In a La Mancha church, the interior colored by light refracted from the windows shifts one readily from the harshness of every-day life to the inducements of belief in transubstantiation.

But can one legitimately claim that the vast La Mancha landscape of four hundred years ago has remained unchanged since Cervantes gave it fictional life in *Don Quixote*? Such an assertion smacks more of a need to fit Cervantes into a particular niche in the diversity of literary refractions than it does to validity. Yet this area of almost twenty thousand square miles is still made up mostly of flat plains dotted with small villages and towns, many of them decimated by repopulation in urban centers. It is true that the formidable contemporary trio—technology, transportation, and architec-ture—have altered some aspects of La Mancha. The diagrammic grid has gained rows of electric and telephone poles; motorized vehicles run on roads and train tracks; building has changed little—ironically what stands out most today is that which comes from Cervantes' time, and Spain's modest economic state since then has not encouraged much building in this area of central plains—structural iron used in construction has been the one substantial change.

Renaissance architecture of note is not hard to find. The road to Almagro, for example, a La Mancha town in which the Calatrava knights established their eseignoral mansions, leads from flat, uninhabited countryside abruptly into the town itself. One drives past a huge walled convent with a beautiful patio established by the knights in the sixteenth century. Opposite it, across an open expanse too unkempt to be called a plaza in a row of modest low houses is an equally modest food place called, inevitably, the Meson Sancho. But Almagro's big surprise lies directly off its superb Plaza Mayor, row upon row of Flemish-inspired three-story dwellings lin-ing the plaza's formally tiled center. Facing the plaza, still in active use, is the Corral de Comedias, the sole remaining open-pit theater of sixteenth-century Europe, a contempo-rary of Shakespeare's Globe Theater in London. Cervantes' plays, including his *entreméses*, were presented here during his lifetime. A Renaissance theater festival is held in the Corral every fall. The theater is somewhat restored, it is˙ true, but after all it is a wooden structure.

The marketplace along the street is a case in point. Here we have no buildings but simply a location. Stalls are set up every Wednesday and Saturday to offer the timeless agronomic staples: cabbages and potatoes, carrots, tomatoes, and greens brought in from surrounding farms by peasants whose dress, stridency of voice, and manner persuade one that Sancho's spirit lives and that the domestic scene remains much the same.

Spain in Cervantes' time was at the zenith of her power; the Golden Age brought bankruptcy and centuries of economic stress in its wake. La Mancha has no place in the tourism that helped Spain's restored economy in this century. Tourists drive south through the long flat stretches of La Mancha, scarcely knowing it is there, en route to the high-rises of the frenetic Mediterranean resorts.

Manchegans seem to possess a curious mélange of the essential qualities of both Don Quixote and Sancho Panza— the knight's courtesies and reverence for tradition, and the squire's rough practicality, gourmandizing, and materialism. Manchegan peasants, farmers, and merchants are sturdily rooted in the rock-bound realities of their strenuous lives—in these they resemble Sancho. But their legendary *cortesia*, their flights of rhetorical extravagance, their deep respect for tradition and customs of the past, link them to the fictional knight errant.

The muleteers, the Yanguesan carriers, and the men in the novel who lived by transporting goods, with their wineskins and rough natures, often encountered Quixote in *ventas* (inns) and on the road. Today's truck drivers of fifteen-ton vehicles, bottles of beer or soda in hand, replace their forerunners at roadside stops and gas stations. Now they can travel from Madrid to the Mediterranean in one day, and the inns are occupied by tourists. The truck drivers are a tough lot: rough spoken and aggressive as their predecessors, but they frequently take courteous pains to advise faster vehicles when it is safe to pass.

Don Quixote's treasured old nag, Rocinante, has become an ancient but trusty automotive vehicle, and Sancho Panza's beloved mule, Dapple, a motorized bicycle. Their owners give them names and form the same sentimental attachement to the machines as the fictional characters did to the animals.

Maritones, the Asturian wench, who was willing to sleep with anyone who propositioned her, is the kind of timeless character who today is the town or village whore, good-natured and priding herself on her honesty.

Quixote's witnessing a corpse being borne by a group of mourners chanting rituals in not unlike today's funerals in small towns, which feature the coffin being borne by mourn-ers through the streets, followed by townspeople and a band playing dirges. One morning recently, I found myself in what seemed like a deserted El Toboso, until I discovered what appeared to be the entire population of the village marching in a long line from the deceased's home to the church.

Just as Don Quixote imagined that an ordinary peasant girl, charmless and even unsightly, could be his beautiful and peerless Dulcinea disguised by enchanters, so the young women of today's La Mancha living in villages and on farms are transformed by makeup and costumes on festival days into creatures of allurement in the eyes of the young bucks.

When I set out on my own quest I'm not sure that I had any idea just how I would ascertain if the spirit of Don Quixote and Sancho Panza still pervaded the region of La Mancha. I soon found that their likenesses were as prevalent as those of political figures in totalitarian countries. Icono-graphically, Quixote is to La Mancha as Lenin is to Russia. And as previously observed, at the entrance of almost every town is a fairly substantial wall or road sign, and on it is the name of the town, its location in La Mancha, and an outline in black of Quixote on his steed.

La Mancha may be the only political region in the world today with the psychological daring to celebrate a deluded fictional figure bent on putting his idealistic world to rights. That this figure is ludicrously ill equipped in every sense to carry out his doomed mission only sharpens the iconic cutting edge.

Countless commercial establishments have taken the names of characters in *Don Quixote*. So comfortable are the Manchegans in their familiarity with the novel that the commercial use of any particular character's name is understood to reflect the quality of the enterprise. Patrons assume that Don Quixote's name on inns or restaurants implies elevated standards of service and cuisine. Sancho's name, on the other hand, is taken to indicate informality—*his* taverns will provide typical fare in large portions at low prices; the interior will be crowded, smoky, noisy, and, in a word, Sanchoesque. Sancho's name adorns not only eating places but bars, tobacconists, roadside pottery stands, gasoline stations, garages, and machine shops.

Even Rocinante has a few garages, but the Manchegans draw the line at Dapple. Dulcinea's name is given to sedate establishments, frequently to shops selling wedding gowns that ignore contemporary fashion and accentuate the bride's romantic version of herself in a cloud of white tulle before a congregation stunned by her ethereal radiance. The town of Herencia sports a location called "La Casa de Maritones." In Puerto Lapice, a recently built windmill carries the name of Bachiller Sanson Carrasco, thereby calling for a more than superficial acquaintance with the novel. The town of Alcazar de San Juan, outdoing its neighbors, has *two* statues in its Plaza Mayor, an equestrian arrangement of Quixote on Rocinante, and, a squire's respectful distance behind it, a statue of Sancho on Dapple.

Throughout La Mancha, Don Quixote wins hands down for pictorial and statuary representations, Sancho for commercial establishments bearing his name. Cervantes himself is held by Manchegans at a dignified remove. He does, after all, come from somewhere else in Spain.

Byron, Proust, and Irving altered the future shape of the places they wrote about, but Cervantes created a bifurcated landscape for his novel. On a surface level stretches the conventional La Mancha that the characters call home, their familiar world of plains and small towns. Beneath that lies the skewed La Mancha, conceived by Cervantes as a refraction of the delusory imagination of Don Quixote. Here the degree of obliquity stems from the magnitude of illusions and misconceptions to which Don Quixote is subject.

Cervantes gave his novel these two landscapes. For the first he seems to have wished the image of the physical place to have passed through the prism of his imagination and emerge as almost an exact reproduction of its physical properties; for the second La Mancha he brilliantly exploited the uses of literary refraction to create a landscape to dazzle one with the bizarre perspectives of his protagonist. Illusion and reality were never placed in better hands.

8

Thoreau's Cape Cod

ARLY IN THE MORNING OF THURSDAY, OTOBER 11, 1849, Henry David Thoreau set off to walk the thirty miles of uninterrupted beach facing the Atlantic at the tip of Cape Cod. A heavy rain was falling. Strong winds, the aftermath of a great storm, lashed the narrow strip of land known as the Lower Cape. Thoreau responded to the weather with the rising spirits of one who made it his business to deal forthrightly with nature. He unfurled his umbrella and strode on.

Under an adjoining umbrella was his friend, William Ellery Channing. An ideal traveling companion, Channing was everything Thoreau was not—impractical, disorganized, amenable. He maintained that he was concerned only with the ethereal and the universal; the particular and definite had no interest for him. Thoreau called him a genius who lacked talent.

No one ever denied Thoreau's talent, and not a few have acknowledged his genius. From his point of view, Thoreau invented nothing. Nature had done it all. His lifelong quest explored the intricacies of nature's multifaceted invention. Man, who thought of himself as nature's supreme achieve-

133

ment, was the single greatest deterrent to Thoreau's research. Man had found a thousand intricate ways to unravel the skein of nature's fabric and Thoreau had little patience with him. Whether at Walden, or in the north woods of Maine, or here on the dunes at Cape Cod, Thoreau sought landscapes empty of man.

Thoreau's reputation has fluctuated with the times. Obscured by Emerson during his lifetime, at the turn of the century he was regarded as a minor literary figure. As the century progressed he became the avowed prototype of those like Gandhi who saw him as an exemplar of passive resistance; he took his place as one of America's major writers; and finally, in the nineteen sixties, he became a cult hero.

An entire generation used him as the model of one who repudiated the establishment, rejected the commerical dross of cities for unsullied nature, and lived in response to the truth of experience. He was turned into a guru, as esthete, a saint, a radical. He was never more misunderstood. He was far from the prototypical dropout: a Harvard graduate, an exacting professional in all his activities—schoolmaster, surveyor, gardener, farmer, naturalist, lecturer, botanist, house painter, traveler, and above all, writer. As an iconoclast, he has been recognized more in kind than in degree. Flinty, unsentimental, tough, his eccentricities were those of a man true to himself.

Thoreau the writer considers nature a challenge. He would like to perceive nature without interference of refraction. He seeks to discover what lies beneath the surface. Unlike Proust, he wants to view the surface unadorned: not hawthorn blossoms, but razor clams are his specimens. His method has the ironic result of calling attention as much to its creator as it does to his subject. Irresistibly drawn to the inductive method, he moves from individual cases to general observations with the persistence of the hungry mosquitoes that pursued him in the Maine woods.

Thoreau visited Cape Cod four times, and his book, *Cape Cod,* published in 1865 three years after his death, stems from the notes that merge the first three visits into one, just as he had incorporated two years into one for *Walden.* But this initial trip in 1849, when Thoreau walked the great beach and the sandbanks for the first time, became the nucleus of *Cape Cod.* Thoreau and Channing had traveled to the Lower Cape by taking the Cape Cod Railroad from Boston to Sandwich, stopping at Bridgewater to "pick up a few arrowheads there." At Sandwich they took a nine-passenger stagecoach to Orleans, where they spent the night at Higgins's Tavern. Here the guests felt "very much as if they were on a sand bar in the ocean." Thoreau spoke characteristically on seasonal Cape Cod: "A storm in the Fall or Winter is the time to visit; a light-house or a fisherman's hut the true hotel. A man may stand there and put all America behind him."

Thoreau's walking attire consisted of a hat (size 7) inside of which he had a special "shelf" made, the better to carry interesting botanical specimens; a topcoat over a brown or greenish three-piece suit; a knapsack especially made with partitions for his books (always a guidebook and one for pressing flowers) and papers, his maps, his sewing materials, both his jackknife and his clasp knife, his compass, his fishing line and hooks, some bread, sugar, salt, and tea. Next to these he placed his spyglass and his measuring tape. He also brought along a treat, "a junk of heavy cake" with plums in it, to reward himself after undue toil.

As the two men approached the rain-drenched shoreline, passing the Eastham Meeting House, they could hear the pounding of the unseen surf. Suddenly Thoreau and Channing found themselves on the edge of a bluff overlooking the Atlantic. This was their first sight of the shoreline they would follow for the next three days until they reached Race Point at the Provincetown tip.

Thoreau's journey of discovery was about to begin.

Thoreau was as meticulous in his description here as in observing Walden Pond.

> Far below us was the beach, from half to a dozen rods in width, with a long line of breakers rushing to the strand. The sea was exceedingly dark and stormy, the sky completely overcast, the clouds still dropping rain, and the wind seemed to blow not so much as the exciting cause, as from sympathy with the already agitated ocean. The waves broke on the bars at some distance from the shore, and curving green and yellow as if over so many unseen dams, ten or twelve feet high, like a thousand waterfalls, rolled in foam to the sand. There was nothing but that savage ocean between us and Europe.

Since the early eighteenth century, residents of the towns (Wellfleet, Truro, Provincetown) facing Cape Cod Bay have referred to this Outer Cape with its unparalleled expanse of dunes and Atlantic beach as the "backside." The towns were built on the bay side to take advantage of the protective harbors; the backside oceanfront dunes and beaches served the townspeople as a barrier on the wilder side of nature.

On that first morning the two men, battling the wind with their umbrellas, began their hike on the sodden sand of the beach itself. Not a sail was in sight along this perilous coastline where frequent shipwrecks cast debris of all kinds up on the sands. Limited visibility persuaded Thoreau and Channing to climb to the top of the dune in order to continue at that height.

"This sand bank," writes Thoreau,

> the backbone of the Cape, rose directly from the beach to the height of a hundred feet or more above the ocean. It was with singular emotions that we first . . . discovered

what a place we had chosen to walk on. On our left, extending back from the very edge of the bank, was a perfect desert of shining sand . . . on our right beneath us, was the beach of smooth and gently sloping sand; next the endless series of white breakers; further still, the light green water over the bar, which runs the whole length of the forearm of the Cape, and beyond this stretched the unwearied and illimitable ocean.

The two men moved from dune to beach and back again, responding to the susceptibility of each in turn. Soon they were in an area of the dunes with small hills and valleys covered in shrubbery, known today as Lecount Hollow in South Wellfleet.

They came to recognize what anyone who attempts to emulate them today soon realizes. There are only two "roads" —as Thoreau called them—the dune bank and the beach. For twenty-eight uninterrupted miles from Nauset to Race Point the dunes and the beach face the Atlantic. The prospect is undomesticated, untenanted, a daunting expanse to lift the spirits. Thoreau wrote: "I had got the Cape under me, as much as if I were riding it bare-backed . . . it cannot be represented on a map, color it as you will; the thing itself, than which there is nothing more like, no truer picture or account; which you cannot go farther and see."

Thoreau and Channing took their time. Thoreau had organized this hike so as to savor the quality of what he might encounter. He had long wanted to see this narrow strip of unprotected land facing the open sea. His sharp eye missed nothing. He came upon strangely shaped strands of seaweed of unexpected colors and textures, "Beautiful sea jellies," large clams, oddly twisted driftwood, mulitcolored pebbles and stones, shells of varied shapes and hues. Overhead flew the mackerel gulls; the sound of their cry is one that Thoreau claims most perfectly captures the impression made by the beach.

The first and only human they encountered that morning was a wrecker, with a grapple and a rope, who said he was looking for tow cloth from the cargo of the ship *Franklin*, wrecked there in the spring.

It was time for lunch. Thoreau collected some damp driftwood reducing it to shavings with his knife, and with these he lighted a fire and cooked one of the large clams on the embers. When the clam was done, "one valve held the meat and the other liquor. Though it was very tough, I found it sweet and savory, and ate the whole with a relish." A relish he would regret that evening, when his stomach rejected this savory offering of nature's beneficence.

The sky cleared in the afternoon, although the wind continued and the breakers ran as high as ever. The two men came to a charity house of a kind that existed until 1872 when they were replaced by Coast Guard life-saving stations. These huts were erected for the benefit of any who might be shipwrecked and find themselves in dire need of shelter. Straw covered the floor of the windowless dwelling, which contained a stove and sometimes a bench. Except perhaps "for one memorable night" such houses stood dark and empty the year around, the gulls screaming above, the roar of the ocean resounding through the rough planks.

Thoreau saw the house as a mock of human charity. In response to Channing's claim that he had not a particle of sentiment, Thoreau demurred, declaring that as far as this Cape Cod hike was concerned he "did not intend this for a sentimental journey."

Thoreau's customary traveling attire often caused others to take him for an itinerant peddlar. In his time, if a traveler were in need of overnight accommodation while away from cities, he knocked on the door of the first likely habitation and offered to pay for his lodging. That first night Thoreau and Channing found themselves in a house built back from the dunes but still within the sound of the sea. Thoreau's host, referred to only as the "Wellfleet Oysterman" in *Cape Cod*, was John Newcomb, then eighty-eight years old (he claimed to have heard the guns fire at Bunker Hill when he was fourteen). His style of conversation, Thoreau writes, was coarse and plain enough to have suited Rabelais. Newcomb hunted, tended his crops, fished, and mended his fences. His trade had been that of a Wellfleet oysterman (on the bay side) and his sons were still engaged in it.

Newcomb couldn't place Thoreau: he was not the first man unable to understand what Thoreau "did." A peddlar? A preacher? A tinker? Thoreau was quick to recognize that he was in the presence of another unconventional, sharply opinionated individual. Newcomb maintained that his wife, Thankful, to whom he had been married for sixty-four years, was "deaf as an adder, and the other (his daughter who lived with them) is not much better. These women are both of them good-for-nothing critturs." Early the next morning, the "old woman of eighty-four winters was already out in the cold morning wind, bareheaded, tripping about like a young girl, and driving up the cow to milk. She got the breakfast, and without noise or bustle."

Thoreau's account of this breakfast is classic Americana:

... the old man resumed his stories, standing before us, who were sitting, with his back to the chimney, and ejecting his tobacco juice right and left into the fire behind him, and without regard to the various dishes which were there preparing. At breakfast we had eels, buttermilk cake, cold bread, green beans, doughnuts and tea. The old man talked a steady stream; and when his wife told him he had better eat his breakfast, he said: "Don't hurry me; I have lived too long to be hurried." I ate of the apple sauce and the doughnuts, which I thought sustained the least detriment from the old man's shots, but my companion refused the apple sauce, and ate of the hot cake and the green beans, which had appeared to him to occupy the safest part of the hearth. But on comparing notes afterward, I told him that the butter-milk cake was particularly exposed, and I saw how it suffered repeatedly, and therefore I avoided it; but he declared that, however that might be, he witnessed that the apple sauce was seriously injured, and had therefore declined that.

The second day was clear and bright. Thoreau and Chan-ning walked from Newcomb's house to Highland Light, a distance of some nine miles. Thoreau examined stones and shells, seaweed, small plants, the carcasses of fish and birds, (on a subsequent Cape Cod walk he tied a dead bird to the spoke of his umbrella and carried it along until he could examine it in detail that night). He even noted the varying degrees of coarseness of the sand itself.

He and Channing "bathed in some shallow within a bar, where the sea covered us with sand at every flux, though it was quite cold and windy." He reports that despite the tanta-lizing prospect of sea bathing, no one went in the water on the Atlantic side, "on account of the undertow and the rumor of sharks." Looking out to sea, Thoreau saw hundreds of boats on it—fishing vessels, sailing schooners, and small dorries.

In Thoreau's time beach detritus was likely to smack of human drama. The numerous shipwrecks cast up not only bodies, but trunks and personal belongings together with bolts of cloth and webbing and other valuables that the residents on the bay side dragged home. After storms, many town dwellers crossed over to wait patiently on top of the dunes to spot the debris drifting toward the shore from the wrecked ships.

Here Thoreau the practical Yankee was at war with the Thoreau who disdained material acquistion. But he "saved, at the cost of wet feet only, a valuable cord and buoy, part of a seine, with which the sea was playing, for it seemed ungracious to refuse the least gift which so great a personage offered you. [I] brought this home and still use it for a garden line."

The only dwellings Thoreau and Channing saw near the water were the small houses adjacent to the Eastham and Truro lighthouses in which the keepers and their families lived. Here accommodation was offered to boarders for $3.50 a week, room and board. On the second night of their journey the two men stayed at the Highland lighthouse (since rebuilt) in the Truro area. Thoreau inspected the lighthouse with the interest of one who was not inexperienced in the art of living alone with nature. From the Highland Light he "could see the revolving light at Race Point, the end of the Cape, about nine miles distant, and also the light on Long Point, at the entrance of Provincetown Harbor, and one of the distant Plymouth Harbor Lights, across the Bay, nearly in range with the last, like a star on the horizon."

He and the lighthouse keeper spoke of the erosion of the narrow strip of land on which they were standing. "I judged," Thoreau writes, "that generally it was not wearing away here at the rate of more than six feet annually. Any conclusions drawn from the observations of a few years or one generation only are likely to prove false, and the Cape may balk expectation of its durability." Despite erosion, the sandbanks in Thoreau's opinion continued to maintain their heights:

Not only the land is undermined, and its ruins carried off by currents, but the sand is blown from the beach directly up the steep bank where it is one hundred and fifty feet high, and covers the original surface there many feet deep. If you sit on the edge you will have ocular demonstration of this by soon getting your eyes full. Thus the bank preserves its height as fast as it is worn away.

The second night was spent more peaceably than the first. Both Thoreau's stomach and the sea had subsided. Early the next morning he was up to see the sun rise out of the ocean. This transcendent experience, nowhere better viewed than from atop a Cape Cod dune, is one of nature's steel traps set to ensnare the amateur writer who imagines that the sunrise offers itself for re-creation in prose. Thoreau knew better. Nature was entitled to extravagances, but Thoreau never confused himself with nature. He was one of its creatures, and he spent a lifetime attempting to simplify his role so that he could find within himself the essence of the credo that less is more.

He and Channing prepared for the final day's walk by "annoint[ing their] shoes faithfully with tallow." The sand and salt water had turned them red and crisp. Their shoes had filled with sand many times during the past two days. Thoreau was pleased that his "best black pants" bore none of the stains or dirt that a customary walk would bring about.

In a geographical area such as Cape Cod—long, narrow, and open to the elements—two men walking for several days are bound to be observed and remarked upon despite the remoteness of the location. Forty-eight hours after Thoreau and Channing set out, the Provincetown Bank was robbed by two men. Speedy emissaries from the town made particular inquiries at the Highland lighthouse concerning Thoreau and Channing. Thoreau remarks that they would probably have been arrested had they not left the Cape soon after their arrival that night in Provincetown. Thoreau's prison record of one July night three years previously for nonpayment of the poll tax thus remained unsullied.

This last day was cold and windy. The sparkling surface of the sea caused the two men to fantasize about the distant land (Galicia? The Bay of Biscay? The coast of Portugal?) that lay hidden beyond the sharply outlined horizon. For three or four miles along the beach they saw no one. A few houses were visible in the distance. Soon to the north, as they traversed the wrist between Truro and Provincetown, they sighted the mackerel fleet pouring around the Cape's end north of them, ten or fifteen miles distant, schooner after schooner, "a city," says Thoreau, "on the water."

From time to time the two men took shelter behind a sand hill. Thoreau saw movement everywhere: the sandpipers running out to the water's edge, the gulls crying overhead, the receding fleet of ships. A fox came to the edge of the bank. The scudding clouds, the flashing light upon the water, the grains of sand whirling in eddies—all was primordial, solitary, evanescent.

"Nothing remarkable was ever accomplished in a prosaic mood," wrote Thoreau. His journal kept him from the dangers of nostalgia; his temperament spared him the pitfalls of prosaic moods. His unsentimental personification of nature reflects his transcendental cast of mind, Walking along the seashore on that last day Thoreau contemplated the immensity of the universe and atavistic emergence of human life from the sea. But he had no use for rhapsodic illusions about the beach.

It is a wild rank place, and there is no flattery in it. Strewn with crabs, horseshoes, and razor clams, and whatever the sea casts up—a vast morgue, where famished dogs may range in packs, and crows come daily to glean the pittance which the tide leaves them. The carcasses of men and beasts together lie stately upon its shelf, rotting and bleaching in the sun and waves, and each tide turns them in their beds, and tucks fresh sand under them. There is naked Nature, inhumanly sincere, wasting no thought on men, nibbling on the cliffy shore where gulls wheel amid the spray.

Naked Nature, inhumanly sincere in this wild rank place, wasting no thought on men, was the kind of Nature that Thoreau treasured. But at days's end, Thoreau had reached his intended destination. He took observation atop a sand hill. "We overlooked Provincetown and its harbor, now emptied of vessels, and also a wide expanse of ocean. As we did not wish to enter Provincetown before night, though it was cold and windy, we . . . walked along the beach again nearly to Race Point, being still greedy of the sea influence."

Contemplating his thirty-mile walk along Cape Cod's outer shore, Thoreau states:

> I do not know where there is another beach in the Atlantic States, attached to the mainland, so long, and at the same time so straight, and completely uninterrupted by creeks or coves of fresh-water rivers or marshes . . . certainly there is none where there is a double way, such as I have described, a beach and a bank, which at the same time shows you the land and the sea, and part of the time two seas.

And what of the future for this spectacular stretch of dunes and beach? Thoreau speculated that in due course "this place will be a place of resort for those New Englanders who really wish to visit the sea side. At present it is wholly unknown to the fashionable world, and probably it will never be agreeable to them." Scathingly, Thoreau made it clear that by "fashionable" he referred to those who vacationed at resorts like Newport where they cared "more for the wine than the brine."

*   *   *

Earlier in the morning than Henry David Thoreau, I set out recently just before sunrise to see what the intervening years had brought to this thirty miles of Cape Cod beach from Eastham to Provincetown. The sky was cloudless, a star-studded moonless night of black intensity already giving way to the rays of a midsummer's sun rising from the sea. I heed Thoreau's warning that this phenomenon does not lend itself to prose description.

The tide was out. I had a wide stretch of flat, hard sand to walk on. The ocean was to my right, the sand dunes rising as high as seventy feet to my left. An occasional gull soared in the northeast wind; three black ducks dived for food underwater half minutes at a time; a few crabs scurried along the shore. They made up the entire complement of the visible world of the living.

Sand, sky, and sea coalesced. Then from atop the dune, sliding and rolling and making their own small contribution to erosion, tumbled Jeremy and Mark. Jeremy is eight, Mark six. Most mornings in the summer we three meet here. Their parents trust me to send them back in time for breakfast. But today they know that I am undertaking the Thoreau walk to see what almost a century and a half has done to this shifting mercurial dot in his closely observed universe.

Thoreau's three-day walk over beach and dune covered almost precisely the area administered today by the Cape Cod National Seashore. Thoreau could walk it now, one imagines, without any serious sense that the terrain had altered or been desecrated by those with more interest in the wine than the brine. But he would be wrong. Everything looks much the same, and everything is different.

Not a grain of sand that Thoreau walked upon is still there. The height and contours of the dunes have altered. The relative widths and dimensions of the beach have changed. It never looked before exactly as it does today, and it will never look exactly this way again.

Jeremy and Mark walk with me for a few miles before turning back. We are old friends who scarcely know one another. We met on the beach, and we have never seen one another elsewhere. We are bonded entirely by our love for this particular world that we perceive in distinctive ways. I see the seascape as ephemeral, fugitive, and haunting; in its image I see my transitory life. They see it as permanent: tides go in and out, the sea rages or smoothes to a veneer of glassy brilliance, the wind stings with flying sand and the sun burns the skin. That's simply the way it is. That's what you find when your parents bring you to the seashore in the summer. It's always this way, it always was and always will be.

The fact that ten thousand years ago vast reaches of ice covered this area is mere talk to Jeremy and Mark. If you tell them that seven thousand years ago Cape Cod, Martha's Vineyard, and Nantucket were all part of the same land mass they will listen to you but the information has nothing to do with their existence. They know, because they are New Englanders, that 360 years ago, in November 1620, Cape Cod looked like salvation to those on the *Mayflower* whose landfall on November 15 persuaded them to follow the shoreline around the Provincetown tip to the relative calm of the bay, a safe harbor, and fresh water. "We ... sat us down and drank our first New England water with as much delight as we ever drunk drink in all our lives."

Jeremy and Mark race one another, barefoot on the hard beach. They fall silent and poke inquisitively into the sand. They search the horizon for ships. They scan the sky for the occasional sight of the Concorde, whose sonic boom heralds its return to human vision. Their actions match one another, set in a curious competitive and yet complementary mode spurred by a sense of rivalry and alliance. They have four older brothers and only here can they escape to a world of their own. Except for me, of course. And I don't impede them in any way. They like me. I listen to them and I see them as they can never see themselves. I love them, but in a few years we will scarcely be acquaintances. They will outgrow me, a part of the process all around them they don't yet comprehend.

In the two hundred years between the Pilgrim landing and Thoreau's walk there were no inhabitants on this Lower Cape backside. Cape Codders established their towns in the relative security of the bay side close to the protected harbors. These magnificent dunes and unparalleled stretches of beach they visited mostly in time of trouble. When, as Thoreau noted, they walked across the peninsula to the dunes after great storms, scanning the horizon all too often to discover not only the detritus of a wrecked ship but human bodies as well, borne by gigantic waves toward the shore. Over a seventy-five-year period, the Boston Weather Bureau reported 160 gales here—that is, storms with continuous winds over thirty-two miles per hour. In Thoreau's lifetime, 140 shipwrecks took place on the sandbars directly off the backside of the Lower Cape.

Now there are none. Freighters ply their way at barely visible distances offshore. No small craft except lobster boats and the occasional sailing vessel are seen on this open-ocean side. You can gaze seaward for a whole day and see scarcely a single ship. The bay side has so many sea craft that the marinas cannot contain them.

Today the backside has some five hundred private dwellings. They all came under the jurisdiction of the National Seashore when it was signed into being in 1961. No new homes can be built. Some of the existing ones will eventually be razed and some will disintegrate with time. But on this thirty-mile walk few dwellings are visible. Even when land was available, few persons were foolish enough to build on the edge of the dune; storms of hurricane force brought their houses tumbling down.

Unlike Thoreau and his three-piece suit, I am wearing shorts for this expedition, but like him I carry a knapsack. In mine are binoculars, a camera, a sweater, sneakers (I am barefoot), and some granola bars. I have no maps, no sewing materials, no fishing line. My umbrella is elsewhere. But then Thoreau on this thirty-mile hike was to spend two nights in lodging and I am spending one night en route at the house of friends in Truro.

"It's mine!" Mark shouted. Jeremy was adamant. "I saw it first." I attempt to adjudicate the case of the discovered kite. And the distinction between that kite and Thoreau's "vast morgue" of a beach is a signal that today's shoreline is tenanted for leisure while his was truly undomesticated. Now we use the beach area for surfing, for swimming, for sunbathing and picnicking. Eighty percent of the beach area is federally owned, preserved in perpetuity. The Park Service administers some six beaches with access to the public, the towns administer four or five others.

These Cape Cod beaches here are relatively low key. They are merely small designated areas in the vast stretch of sanded shoreline. In June, a few wooden lifeguard stands are placed on the sand and parking lots are maintained beyond the dune rises. A token admission fee is charged. The water is always cold. Surfers in wetsuits can remain in it for hours, but conventional swimmers have at best a bracing and brief affair with the surf.

When beachcombing, Thoreau found what ships had disposed of; we find what humans have left behind. Plastic: in one form or another, often in colors of repellent hue. Cans. A number of single sneakers who have lost their mates. Boxes. Cartons. We have turned the beach into a residual playground repository. Thoreau's beach was dramatic in its shipwreck implications; ours is comedic in its overtones of indolence.

But as I walk along I see that the designation of seashore

beaches on Cape Cod maps is misleading. Vast spaces stretch between these spots, and unless the weather is warm and sunny the beaches themselves are apt to be deserted. To my left I see the sand blowing from the topmost point of a dune rising perhaps sixty feet. Parts of this scarp are ribbed; layers of sand, pebbles, clay, and moraine are exposed. A great storm in February 1978 altered the face once more of Thoreau's dunes, and metamorphosed areas of land mass to sea floor.

During that ferocious storm winds peaked at ninety-two miles an hour, and combined with a new moon's high tide, produced waves that surged on a level some fourteen and a half feet above mean low water. Most of the wind-built dunes at Nauset Spit were reduced to low mounds; now they barely rise above high tide to separate Nauset Marsh from the sea. Some houses, their foundations eroded, had to be lifted by cranes off the dunes. The owners of houses damaged by the storm resolutely replaced them on new and equally vulnerable foundations. But the self-evident changes brought by such storms are accompanied by more subtle ones: the erosion caused an overhang that traces the top of the dunes where the long grass ends. Every day a sliding to the beach of sand and soil takes place. Strong winds create a kind of sand-fall, visible (as it was to Thoreau) to the most casual observer. Great storms are immediately devastating, but they also carry with them an insidious long-term acceleration of erosion. The Cape has two distinct types of storms: northeasters, whose strong winds with heavy rain or snow can produce abnormally high tides that erode the beaches; and storms of tropical origin with winds of hurricane force, one of which occurs about every two years in late summer or fall.

Thoreau was right. "Any conclusion drawn from the observations of a few years or one generation only are likely to prove false, and the Cape may balk expectation of its durability." But he was mistaken in his assumption that the sand blown from the beach directly up the steep dune bank served to preserve the height of the bank as fast as it is worn away.

Beyond the immediate erosional vulnerability of this stretch of Cape Cod National Seashore oceanfront is the fact of the worldwide rise in sea level that necessarily accompanies the retreat of continental glaciers. The thin inarguable shoreline has been creeping inland since glacial retreat began. A study indicates that the rate of sea-level rise at Cape Cod was about ten feet per one thousand years following the Cape's deposition until about two thousand years ago. Since that time the level of the sea has continued to rise, but at about one-third its former rate, a little more than three feet per one thousand years. The average slope of the continental border is approximately one vertical foot for each one thousand horizontal feet. This means that for every foot the sea level rises (vertically), it would spread one thousand feet over the land (horizontally) if the inclining continental border were perfectly smooth without islands, valleys, hills, and other configurations such as Cape Cod. At present rates, the sea would be encroaching upon the land, if it were a smooth plain, at the rate of about three horizontal feet per year. (Thoreau had estimated that the beach area "was not wearing away here at the rate of more than six feet annually.")

In September 1973 the National Park Service announced that it would no longer try to control shoreline processes everywhere along the coastline within its jurisdiction. This policy stemmed from scientific studies combined with a history of costly failure at controlling eroding shorelines.

Close to the point where Thoreau and Channing first viewed the "savage" ocean, Marconi erected his wireless station a half century later. From this spot the first transatlantic messages in Morse code were exchanged with Poldhu, England. Within months the Cape Cod wireless station was relaying European messages to the *New York Times*. Today, near the cliff where Marconi's high antenna towers once stood is a small sign that reads: "At this point the sea has carved its way inland more than 170 feet since Marconi built his wireless station in 1902."

The beach proper is now a surfer's beach, the waves flecked with black dots of wetsuited women and men skimming the crests of the breakers as their brightly colored surfboards race toward the shore. That sight might have pleased Thoreau more than any other should he see his beach today.

We had now walked for several miles, sometimes together, more often straggling. Jeremy and Mark wanted to accompany me for the entire walk but their parents vetoed the idea: "With you two along it will take him weeks to get there." Jeremy now goes into the icy water up to his waist. His teeth are chattering, his blond hair blowing in the chill wind. He tries to persuade Mark that the water is "great" for swimming. Mark hauls a log down to the water's edge, embedding a large splinter in his thumb. I am beginning to understand their parents' veto. Breakfast is waiting. They wish me well. "See ya. Take care." "You don't look like Thoreau but you'll probably make it," Mark says. Soon I lose sight of them as they disappear over the edge of the dune, one trailing far behind the other.

The day is cloudless. I come to Newcomb Hollow, the northernmost of Wellfleet's town beaches. Unlikely as it seems, John Newcomb's many-windowed clapboard house still stands today well back from the dunes but within the sound of the sea. It is privately owned. Newcomb died at ninety-five, buried in the Wellfleet cemetery to take his place among a remarkable number of gravestones inscribed with ages beyond eighty.

Absurdly close to the spot where Thoreau records that he and Channing bathed in some shallow within a bar is the beach area near Truro known as the Free Beach, a site of local contention between those who claim it as a nude beach and the authorities who oppose it. Thoreau and Channing started something.

I no longer have the beach to myself. In designated beach areas the shoreline is crowded. Midafternoon comes on. I take a long swim, riding the waves again and again to the shore. The beach surface, now that the tide is in, is narrow, and soft sand is heavy to walk on. I am glad to climb the dune and set off toward my friends' house, fairly confident that at breakfast we would not have eels, green beans, and any version of the Newcomb applesauce.

The next morning is partially cloudy, white flecks in a distant blue. Thoreau's three-piece suit would have served me better than my shorts. The wind blows in chill from a choppy sea. Above me a plane, too high in the sky to distinguish, leaves a long, thin, white contrail that soon loses itself in the clouds. Underfoot, the ruts of sharply etched tire marks of the beach patrol jeep are gradually obliterated as the incoming tide runs over the sand. All is primordial, solitary, evanescent.

Climbing the dune bank, I walk along its surface. Here I have a sweeping view of the long swath of beach and the sea far below to the right. Inland the terrain strangely resembles a horizontal version of the plant growth on the side of a great mountain. First, corresponding to the area well above the timber line, there is dune grass, patches of deep green moss (fed by frequent fogs), both on a coarse sandy base. Moving inland, we come upon small tough shrubs, abundant poison ivy, knee-high plants with sharp bristles, and beyond the stunted fir trees leading to a distant stretch of trees and vegetation of conventional height.

The area is alive with wildflowers: yellow and white daisies, buttercups, the tall flame-red "fire" plant, swamp lilies, cornflowers, Queen Anne's lace—but foremost and famously, two varieties of wild roses. The first of these is the single-petaled variety, whose rose hips are used for medicinal and culinary purposes; and the other is the exquisitely formed dune rose that blooms at the end of June and lasts until mid-July. Blueberry bushes abound; nearby cranberry bogs provide generous harvests.

The most common animal here is not the squirrel but the rabbit, shaded to match the sand, with a white bobtail that catches the eye. In the underbrush and shrubbery I spy three foxes, two pups and a mother, who takes a defensive stand and challenges me. One bark, and then silence. Another bark. I stand transfixed. She is cautious but not fearful. No traps or guns are known to her or her kind since 1961. Some thirty-six species of mammals are said to be found on Cape Cod, although few are present in any number. Apart from the cottontail rabbits, the white-tailed deer are the most common. I have seen skunks, muskrats, and once, an otter.

Down there on my right, beneath the surface of the cold, unpolluted sea were swimming a multitude of fish: striped bass, bluefish, flounder, haddock, tuna, and the namesake of the location, the ubiquitous cod. Unwary lobsters find themselves trapped and taken up once a day by energetic fishermen who seem indifferent to weather conditions. I have seen whales spouting in the distance, schools of dolphin, and sometimes for two or three days a number of small sharks are washed up on the beach with the surf; I do not know what kills them.

As Thoreau found, it is tough going along the ridge of the dunes. Sometimes in the deep dune grass one comes upon snakes. I prefer the beach and I do what I know I shouldn't be doing: I sitz-ski down the dune bank, an exhilarating slide made all the more so by closing my eyes to the dune preservation I should be respecting.

Back down on the beach I come upon the shells of horseshoe crabs, one of the last direct descendants of the Paleozoic. And hideous they are. Few shells are found on this backside. Jeremy and Mark collect sand dollars and hang them on a shrub next to their house. But shellfish are mostly on the bay side: species include quahog (cherry stone, little neck, and chowder sizes), streamer or soft-shell clams, sea or hen clams, and some mussels. Oysters are harvested in Wellfleet, and bay scallops are part of the commerical seafood harvest.

Waterfowl are the most important game bird here. The coast of Cape Cod is a wintering area for vast flocks: half a million American eider have been counted, as well as white-winged scoters, Canada geese, black ducks, and a few brants. Gulls swarm—herring, ring-billed, black-backed—and the sandpipers run back and forth as the feathered accompaniment to the ebb and flow of water at the line between sea and land.

Reaching the magnificent rolling Provincetown dunes I climb, like Thoreau, to take observation atop a sand hill. In the Provincetown harbor are many vessels, sailing and motorized, as well as boats for sightseeing and whaling cruises, and in dock the large Boston-Provincetown ferry steamer. Unlike Thoreau, I did wish to enter Provincetown before night, and I confess to being no longer "greedy of the sea influence." I have a painful sunburn, a blister on my right foot, and a number of insect bites to remind me of my portion of the walk in the dune grass. I knew that I would enjoy a cold beer with as much delight as I ever drunk drink in all my life.

Thoreau's beach has gone. In his prescient way he was right: ". . . this place will be a place of resort for those New Englanders who really wish to visit the sea-side." As a resort for vacationers it has become cultivated, domesticized, regulated, subjected to restrictions of access, and forbidden to anyone who wishes to spend the night on its sands. It remains a gift of nature's bounty, breathtaking in its sweep and contours. We are laudably preserving our national heritage, but "rank" has given way to "tame." "Naked Nature, inhumanly sincere" has been clothed and tamed. But only, Thoreau whispers, for a cosmic moment.

Taking Thoreau's walk today, one can see his world through one's own refracted vision. His prose is as bracing as the chill of a morning Cape Cod sea breeze, his eye as sharp as the needle he carried for minor repairs, and his love for the physical world in which he found himself is always saved from even a whiff of sentimentality or self-pity by his flinty nature. Passing as it does through the prism of Thoreau's imagination, the image of this physical world is stripped of artifice and in the intensity of his vision nothing is spared, least of all himself.

Bibliography

The nine writers in this book have spawned cottage industries for biographers and literary critics, while dramatists, artists, journalists, and translators have found them to be a source of gratifying career enhancement. Academia employs them as foundation stones to persuade students to produce a frightening number of book reports, term papers, essays, theses, and doctoral dissertations, almost all of them unread except by the student and teacher, and often by only one or the other. A complete bibliography would be as long as this book is long, too vast to annotate, too indigestible to swallow, too pointless to contemplate.

Homer

The Iliad and *The Odyssey* as the root works of Western literature for some three thousand years have been translated into English—in the early Renaissance years from Latin—many times. Perhaps the most frequently read modern English poetic translation is Richmond Lattimore's. A contemporary prose translation of *The Iliad* by E. V. Rieu, published by Penguin Books, has deservedly sold well over a million copies; I have used it here. Michael Wood's *In Search of the Trojan War*, New American Library, a companion volume to the PBS Television series, makes what the English call "a good read" with respect to Homer's creation of the City of Troy.

Chaucer

Chaucer's *Troilus and Cressida,* his only full-length completed work, is untranslatable. His Middle English is just distant enough from present-day language to beguile the unwary translator into believing that the impossible is attainable. Chaucer's deft and witty play of language, his pseudo-naïveté, his own amusement at the limitations of his "rhyme royale" poetic form, and his indifference to a protracted medieval narrative pace, all lay traps for the modern translator. Nevill Cogill, in his 1985 Penguin translation, ensnares himself but manages to survive. I have alternated his translation, when appropriate, with Chaucer's Middle English. A reading of Boccaccio's *Il Filostrato* offers both a lesson on Chaucer's indebtedness (never acknowledged) to Boccaccio as source, and a sharp reminder of the power of Chaucer's creative imagination in shaping, refining, and giving glorious life to the material.

Proust

Scholars make fine distinctions between the classic C. K. Scott-Moncrieff seven-volume Modern Library 1951 edition of *Remembrance of Things Past* and that of Terence Kilmartin's three-volume Random House 1981 edition. Clearly, reading the original *À la recherche du temps perdu*, Editions Gallimard, Paris, 1954, is best of all. In writing about Combray and Illiers, I have found the following of particular interest: George D. Painter's *Proust: The Early Years,* Little, Brown & Co., 1959, with photographs, maps of Illiers, and perceptive biographical observations; *Proust's Binoculars,* Roger Shattuck's 1967 Vintage study of memory, time, and recognition; Jean-François Revel's *On Proust,* 1972, Open Court, Lasalle, Ill., in particular his chapter on Montaigne and Proust; Samuel Beckett's *Proust,* Grove Press, 1931, based on his theory that Proust had a bad memory ("the man with a good memory does not remember anything because he does not forget anything"); Howard Moss's *The Magic Lantern of Marcel Proust,* Grosset & Dunlap, 1962, a brilliant critical study; the Prentice-Hall collection of critical essays, edited by René Girard; and *A Reader's Guide to Marcel Proust,* Farrar, Straus and Cudahy, Milton Hindu's 1962 analysis of various motifs entwined in Proust's vast novel.

Byron

At the turn of the century (1898–1904) John Murray of London published the 13-volume collection of Byron's poetry, journals, and letters. Since then the Everest of books and articles on Byron threatens to disappear from sight in literary cloudland. Leslie Marchand's 1957 biography published by Knopf, and volume 8 of his *Byron's Letters and Journals* published by John Murray are key works when writing about Byron's visit to Sintra. *Selected Prose,* edited by Peter Gunn, Penguin, 1973, has many of Byron's letters together with an excellent introduction. W. H. Auden's comments on Byron in

The Selected Poetry and Prose of Byron published by New American Library in 1966 are wry and to the point. Peter Quennell edited *Byron, A Self Portrait, Letters and Diaries, 1798–1824,* published by Scribners. Two perceptive books on Byron are Iris Origo's *The Last Attachment,* Scribners, 1942, and Michael K. Joseph's *Byron the Poet,* Gallancz, London, 1964. Louis Crompton's *Byron and Greek Love: Homophobia in 19th-Century England,* University of California Press, 1984, examines the homophobic climate of Byron's time as well as the homosexual aspect of Byron's nature.

Dostoyevsky

Dostoyevsky's collected works are the best bibliographical support for understanding his refracted view of Florence. His letters, translated and with an introduction by Avrahm Yarmolinsky *(Letters of Fyodor Dostoevsky)* Horizon Press, 1961, include most of the important material I have used here. Some of the letters are superseded by the four-volume *Complete Letters,* edited by David Lowe and Rojnold Meyer, translated by Ethel Colburn Mayme. I found *Dostoevsky Reminiscences,* by Anna Dostoyevsky, translated by Beatrice Stillman, Liveright, 1977, indispensible for providing some balance to Dostoyevsky's categorical repudiation of Florence. This is an intimate portrait by Dostoyevsky's extraordinarily patient, somewhat plodding, loving, and attentive wife who consistently places her late husband in a favorable light; her marriage to a tormented genius twenty-five years her senior seemed destined to produce a martyr but brought forth a marvel. Of particular biographical and critical interest is the multivolume work-in-progress on Dostoyevsky by Joseph Frank, being published by Princeton University Press.

Twain

Twain's critique of Venice appears in *The Innocents Abroad*, New American Library, 1966. The book is essentially a collection of Twain's newspaper articles, substantially revised and edited by Twain and Bret Harte. Everyone likes to write about Twain; he provides critics with one punch line after another. Serious academic critics of Twain tend to find his duality an irresistible platform for biographical and literary analysis.

Irving

Washington Irving has been patronized more than any other American writer of quality. Every critic wants Irving to do better at whatever the critic thinks is crucial to literary distinction. Stanley Williams in his exhaustive two-volume biography (Oxford University Press) is particularly exasperated with Irving for not being someone else. Irving's *Tales of the Alhambra* continues to shape both the future of the monumental site and the itineraries of millions of travelers.

Cervantes

Spain's most famous prose writer invites critics to emphasize bifurcation of both theme and characterization in their writings on *Don Quixote*. Emboldened, they proceed to view *Don Quixote* as emblematic not merely of Spain, but of life itself. Somehow the novel has managed to survive. Martin Nosick's chapter on "The Myth of Don Quixote" in his *Miguel de Unamuno: The Agony of Belief,* Princeton University Press, illuminates both Cervantes and Unamuno. Cervantes lends himself to translation into English only a little less unsuccessfully than Shakespeare into Spanish.

Thoreau

Thoreau's *Cape Cod,* Thomas Crowell, contains most of the material referred to here in the discussion of his walk from Eastham to Provincetown. Critics would love to find a convenient label, a neat category, an immovable plaque for Thoreau, but he continues to elude them. He made himself comfortably at home in his unconventional world, and he did the same with his prose.

Index

Academy Museum, The (Galleria dell'Accademia), 68
Achaens, The, 11
Achilles, 13, 15
Acropolis, The, 12–13
Adrestus, 13
Adventures of Huckleberry Finn (Twain), 107
Aegean Islands, 15
Africa, 54
Agamemnon, 14–15
Agisthus, 15
Albacete (Spain), 115
Albania, 51, 56
Albert, Prince Consort, 52
Alcazaba, The (Alhambra), 90
Alcazar de San Juan (Spain), 131
Alexandrine, 9
Alfonso, King Henriques, 44
Algeria, 36–37, 39
Algiers, 68
Alhambra, The, 77–95, 108, 121, 124
Alhambra, The (Irving), 77–78, 81–88, 90

Ali Pacha, Grand Vizier, 51
Almagro (Spain), 119, 128
Alps, The, 76
Alta California (San Francisco), 97–98, 107
Ambassadors, Hall of (Alhambra), 80
America/American, 75, 78, 82, 90, 92, 98, 101–102, 105–108, 111, 134–139, 154
Amiot, Elisabeth, 36–38
Amiot, Jules, 36–37, 39
Amiot, Germaine, 37
Amis de Marcel Proust, Les, 37–38
Amis de Combray, Les, 37
Andalusia, 78, 81, 125
Andromache, 13
Antenor, 14, 18
Antigone, 19–20
Apollo, 9
Arab/Arabic, 39, 60, 77, 79, 81–82, 86, 90, 93–95, 125
Argamasilla de Alba (Spain), 118–121
Argos, 10

163

Arkansas, 98
Asia/Asian, 90
Astyanax, 14
Athena, 13
Atlantic Ocean, 133, 135–137, 140,
   144
Auden, Wystan Hugh, 47
Auteuil, (France), 38

Baden-Baden (Germany), 74
Bankers, Guild of (Florence), 69
Baptistry, The (Florence), 68
Bargello Museum, The (Florence),
   67
Beauce (France), 35
Beckford, Sir William, 45, 49, 51,
   53, 54, 58–59
Benoit de Sainte-Maure, 16
Berlin, 74, 76
Bible, The, 115
Biscay, Bay of, 143
Black Sea, 9, 24
Bloch (Proust), 26
Boabdil, Mohammed X1, 82–84, 94
Boccaccio, Giovanni, 16
Boston, 135, 147, 154
Bowers, Ambassador Claude, 91
Bridgewater, Mass., 135
Britain/British, 16, 49
Brothers Karamazov, The, 72
Browning, Elizabeth Barrett, 63
Browning, Robert, 63
Brunelleschi, Filippo, 105
Bunker Hill, 139
Byron, Lord George Gordon, 35,
   43–51, 53–60, 77, 89, 103–104,
   115, 132
Byzantium/Byzantine, 102

Calatrava, Knights of, 125–126, 128
Calchus, 17–19
Calzada de Calatrava (Spain), 125
Cambridge University, 49
Canada, 154
Canale della Giudecca (Italy), 98

Cape Cod, 133–138, 140–150,
   153–155
Cape Cod (Thoreau), 135, 139
Cape Cod National Seashore, 145,
   147, 150
Capuchin, 44, 59
Carey & Lea, 88
Carrasco, Bachiller Sanson (Cer-
   vantes), 131
Casa Guidi, 63
Cascais, 52
Castiglione, Conte, Baldassare,
   60
Castile, 118
Catholic/Catholicism, 100, 104, 106
Cavaleiros, Estralagem dos (Portu-
   gal), 57
Caxton, William, 16
Cervantes, Saavedra, 115–120, Mi-
   guel de, 122, 124–129, 132
Channing, William Ellery, 133,
   135–142, 150–152
Charles V, Emperor, 79, 85, 90–91
Chartres, 35, 36
Chateaubriand, François, 89, René
   de, 94
Chaucer, Geoffrey, 7–8, 16–23, 61,
   80, 115
Chekhov, Anton, 11
Cheval Blanc, Rue (France), 40
Childe Harold's Pilgrimage
   (Byron), 43, 46–49, 51, 56–58, 88
Chiliwaukee, Iowa, 119
Chios, 9
Christ/Christian, 17, 23, 44, 49, 79,
   117, 127
Chronicle of the Conquest of Granada
   (Irving), 78
Clemens, Samuel, 97, 110, 112–113
Clytemnestra, 15
Ciudad Real, (Spain), 115
Coast Guard, 138
Colares (Portugal), 52
Cologne, 74
Columbus, Christopher, 78, 98

Combray, 25–31, 33, 36–40, 43, 61, 93
Concorde, 146
Connecticut, 93
Conquest of Granada, The, 86
Consuerga (Spain), 126
Convention of Cintra, 49, 59
Cook, Francis, 53–54
Cordoba (Spain), 95
Cork convent (Portugal), 44–45, 58–59
Corral de Comedias (Spain), 128–129
Cosimo I, 69
Courtly Love, 18–20
Courtier, The (Castiglione), 60
Cressida, 16–23
Crime and Punishment (Dostoyevsky), 62, 69–70, 75
Cuenca, (Spain), 115

Dalrymple, Sir Hew, 46
Dante Alighieri, 17, 117, 130–131
Dapple (Cervantes), 117, 130–131
Dardanus, 19
Dares Phygius, 16
Darro Valley (Spain), 86
De Excidio Trojae Historia (Dares Phygius), 16
Deiphebus, 20
Diary of a Writer (Dostoyevsky), 73
Dickie, James, 82, 93–94
Dictys Cretenis, 16
Diderot, 66
Diomede, 14
Disney, Walt, 43
Dolgorouki, Prince Dmitri Ivanovich, 78, 81, 85, 87
Dolon, 13
Don Juan (Byron), 59
Dostoyevsky, Fyodor Mikailovich, 61–76, 87, 115, 117
Dostoyevsky, Anna Grigorevna, 61, 64–68, 70–72

Dostoyevsky, Paul, 64
Dostoyevsky, Lyubov, 72
Dostoyevsky, Sonya Alexandrovna, 65, 67, 70
Dostoyevsky, Donya Mikailovna, 73
Dostoyevsky, Reminiscences (Anna Dostoyevsky), 64, 67
Dostoyevsky, Words and Days (Yarmolinsky), 74
Don Quixote (Cervantes), 115, 118, 128, 131
Don Quixote, 115, 117–127, 129–132
Dresden (Germany), 71–72, 74, 76
Dulcinea, 118–119, 122–123, 130–131
Duomo, The, 68, 105

East/Easterners, 100
Eastham Meeting House (Mass.), 135, 141, 145
Eden, 43, 47, 51, 53, 55–56, 60
Elizabeth of Parma, 85
Elysium, 47
Emerson, Ralph Waldo, 106, 134
England/English, 8, 16, 17, 20, 21, 28, 45, 49–50, 53, 57, 60, 73, 76, 84
English Bards and Scotch Reviewers, 49
Ephemeris Belli Trojani (Dictys), 16
Ernestine (Proust), 38
Eswege, Baron, 53
Estoril (Portugal), 52
Estremadura (Portugal), 46, 52
Eugenie, Empress Marie, 36
Euripides, 16
Europe, 15, 45–46, 50–51, 54, 59–60, 62, 75, 85, 90, 93, 97–98, 100, 108–109, 128, 136, 150
Fall of the House of Usher, The (Poe), 80
Ferdinand V, King, 82, 93
Ferrell, Sarah, 39
Fiero, Abbotof, 126

Fifth Avenue, New York City, 111
Filostrato, Il (Boccaccio), 16
Finland, 70
Flanders/Flemish, 128
Florence, 61–63, 65–76, 87, 117
France/French, 20, 25, 36, 39, 40, 46, 49, 72, 75, 82, 84–85, 106
S/S Franklin, 138
Franciscan, 79
Francoise, (Proust), 26, 38
Françoise le Champi, 38

Galantiere, Lewis, 26
Galicia, 143
Galignani, A. & W., 88
Gautier, Theophile, 90
Generalife (Alhambra), 85–87
Geneva, 65–66, 74–75
Genoa, 74
Geoffrey of Monmouth, 17
Germany, 62–63, 65, 72, 76
Gandhi, Mahatma, 134
Ghiberti, Lorenzo, 68
Gibraltar, 46
Gildemeester, Daniel, 59
Glaucus, 14
Globe Theater, 128
Gogol, Nicolai, 118–119
Golden Age, (Spain), 89, 129
Gothic, 45, 56
Gower, John, 17
Granada, 77–78, 84, 87, 90–91, 93, 95, 126
Grand Canal, 98–99, 103
Grand Hotel d'Europe, 98, 101
Grand Tour, 50
Greece/Grecian, 45–46, 51, 59, 75
Greeks, 7–8, 10, 13–15, 16, 17, 19
Grigioli, Countess, 104
Guermantes, 26, 33, 35, 37
Guermantes way, 31, 33–34
Guicciardina, Via (Florence), 62, 66
Gypsy, 86, 94

Hamlet, 117
Harpers, 89
Harrow, 49
Harte, Bret, 100, 108
Hartford, Conn., 110–111
Harvard University, 118–119, 134
Hassarlik (Turkey), 18
Hector, 12–14
Hecuba, 7, 13
Helen, 11–14, 20–21
Hera, 10, 17
Herencia (Spain), 131
Hermosilla, Don Joseph de, 118
Herodotus, 9
Hieronymite, 49
Higgins Tavern (Mass.), 135
Highland Light (Mass.), 140–142
Historia Regum Britanniae, 17
History of New York, The (Irving), 78, 82
Hobhouse, John, 51, 54, 58–59
Hodgson, Francis, 46
Holy Land, The, 88
Holy Week, 29
Homer, 7–16, 18–21, 23, 61, 115
Hudson Valley, 81
Hugo, Victor, 90

Iberia, 115
Iceland/Icelandic, 88
Idiot, The (Dostoyevsky), 62–63
The Iliad, 9–10, 15, 18
Il Filostrato, 16
Ilium, 10, 13–14
Illiers, 25–26, 29, 35–40, 61, 93, 97
India, 52–53
Innocents Abroad, The (Twain), 100, 106–109
Ionia/Ionian, 15
Ios, 9
Irving, Washington, 77–95, 108, 115, 121, 124, 132
Isabella, I, Queen, 82, 93
Islam/Islamic, 88

Italy/Italian, 16, 62–63, 67–68, 74, 76, 92, 101, 104–106, 119
Izmir, 9

Jacques, St. (Proust), 37, 39
James, St. of Compostella, 27
Janus, 45
Jeremy, 145–146, 148, 151, 153
Joannina, (Greece), 51, 56
Joseph, M.K., 50
Justice, Tower of, 91

Karamazov, Fyodor Pavlovich, 71
Karamazov, Ivan Fyodorovich, 75
Kasten, Maurice, 51
Kilmartin, Terence, 25, 28

La Mancha, 115–120, 122–132
Last of the Abencerrajes, The (Chateaubriand), 90
Latin, 16
Lawrence, Hotel, 57
Lear, 117
Lecount Hollow, Mass., 137
Légion d'Honneur, 36
Legrandin (Proust), 26
Lenin, Vladimir Illyich, 131
Léonie, Aunt (Proust), 28, 30–31, 36–37, 40, 93, 112, 123
Lepanto, Battle of, 116, 120
Le Roman de Troie, 16
Lindaraxa (Alhambra), 85
Lions, Court of (Alhambra), 86
Lisbon, 43, 45–46, 49, 52, 56, 59
Loggia di Mercato Nuovo, 69
Loire (river), 39
Lollius, 16
London, 17, 74, 128
Long Point, 141
Lucerne, 74

Madonna, 38
Madonnadella Sedia, 68, 74
Madrid, 78, 121–122, 130
Maine, 134

Mall (Combray), 33
Manuel I, King, 45
Manueline, 45, 52
Marcel (Proust's narrator), 26–27, 29–38
Marconi, Marchese Guglieimo, 150–151
Marfa, 45
Mark, 145–146, 151, 153
Maria II, Queen, 52
Marialva, Marquis de, 45, 49, 57, 59
Maritones (Cervantes), 130–131
Martha's Vineyard, (Mass.), 146
Mayflower, 146
Medici, The, 106
Mediterranean, The, 68, 101, 125, 129–130
Medrano, Cave of, 120–121
Mello e Castro, Caetano de, 53
Menelaus, 11, 13–14
Méséglise way, 30–31, 33–34, 38
Michelin, 57
Middle Ages, The, 16, 53, 62, 106
Milan, 66, 74, 76
Midwestern, 100, 108
Mississippi, The, 107
Monserrate, 45, 49, 53–54, 58
Montjovain (Proust), 32
Moor/Moorish, 44–45, 52, 77, 79, 84–85, 88, 90, 125, 129
Moore, Thomas, 89
Moslem, 79, 126
Museo de los Tiros (Spain), 93
Myrtles, Court of (Spain), 86
Mycenae, 10

Nabokov, Vladimir, 118–119
Nantucket, Mass., 146
Napoleon, 82, 84
National Park Service, 150
Nauset Beach, Mass., 137, 149
Navarrate, 86
Newcomb, John, 139–140, 151
Newcomb, Thankful, 139

New England/New Englanders, 112, 144, 146, 154
Newport, R.I., 54, 144
Newstead, 50
Newstead Abbey, 89
New York City, 78, 97, 111
New York Times, The, 39, 111, 150
Norman, 35
Norman Conquest, 20
North Africa, 88
Norton Critical Edition, 62

Odyssey, The, 9
Odysseus, 13
Orient/Oriental, 58, 60, 88, 89, 101
Orientales, Les (Hugo), 90
Origo, Iris, 50
Orleans, Mass., 135
Ovid, 23

Painter, George, D., 40
Palace, Royal, of Sintra, 45, 57
Palacio de Seteais, Hotel (Portugal), 57, 59
Palladian, 17
Pandar, 19–22
Panza, Sancho, 117, 119–120, 123, 128–132
Parador San Francisco (Spain), 91
Paris, 11–12, 13, 17
Paris (France), 26, 35, 74–75, 88
Peasants Revolt, 17
Pena, Palacio de, 52–53, 57
Penha, Nossa Senhora de (Portugal), 44–45, 48, 51–52
Peninsular Wars, 82
Perchamps, Rue des (Combray), 33, 35, 39
Persia, 36
Petrarch, Francesco, 17
Philadelphia, 88
Philip V, King, 85
Plaze de los Aljibes (Spain), 90
Piazza della Signorini (Italy), 68
Pisistratus, 9

Pitti Palace (Italy), 62–63, 66, 68
Plymouth, Mass., 141
Poe, Edgar Allan, 80
Poldhu (England), 150
Ponte Vecchio (Italy), 62
Pont-Vieux (Combray), 33
Portugal, 43–46, 48–49, 54–55, 57–59, 143
Poseidon, 10, 15
Possessed, The (Dostoyevsky), 79
Pousada de Lord Byron, 57
Pre Catalan (Combray), 39
Preveza (Greece), 46
Priam, 7, 10–13, 14–15, 18, 20
Princess Elizabeth, The, 45
Protestant/Protestantism, 100–101, 104, 106
Proust, Marcel, 25–41, 43, 61, 93, 112, 115, 123, 132, 134
Proust, Dr. Adrien, 36
Proust, Elisabeth, 36–38
Proust, Louis, 36
Proust, Robert, 36
Proust, Rue Docteur (Combray), 37, 40
Proust: The Early Years (Painter), 40
Provincetown, Mass., 135–136, 141–146, 154
Puerto Lapice (Spain), 119, 121–122, 131
Putnam, Samuel, 118

Quaker City, The, 97, 106, 108–109

Rabelais, François, 139
Race Point, Mass., 136–137, 141, 144
Raphael, 68
Raskolnikov, Rodion Romanovich, 70, 75
Recherche du temps perdu, à la, 40
Recuyell of the Historyes of Troy, 16
Redding, Conn., 111

Remembrance of Things Past, 25–26, 35–36, 43
Renaissance, 16, 19, 45, 52, 59, 60, 62, 79, 85, 94, 106, 119–120, 128
Revel, Jean-Francois, 35
Rip Van Winkle, 78, 92–93
Rocinante (Cervantes), 117, 120, 130–131
Roman de Troie, Le (Sainte-Maure), 16
Romanesque, 37
Romantic/Romanticism, 43–45, 48, 50–51, 53, 60, 79, 94
Rome/Roman, 17, 76, 116
Roughing It (Twain), 110
Roussky Viestnik, 71
Royal Academy, (Spain), 118
Ruskin, John, 102
Russian Messenger, (Roussky Viestnik,) 65
Russia/Russian, 62–63, 66–69, 74–75, 78, 131

Sabonea, Maria Antonia, 80
Saint-Esprit, Rue de (Combray), 31, 37
Saint-Hilaire (Combray), 26, 29–31, 33, 36
St. John of Jerusalem, 126
St. Mark's (Venice), 101–102
St. Petersburg, 61, 69–70, 75
Sainte-Maure, Benoît de, 16
Salvatierra Castle (Spain), 126
San Francisco Monastery (Spain), 97
San Lorenzo Library (Florence), 68
Sand, George, 38
Sandwich, Mass., 135
Santa Cruz, Marquis de, 120
Santa Maria del Fiore (Florence), 68
Sarpedoun, 22
Sarya (Dostoyevsky), 71
Saxe-Coburg-Gotha, Ferdinand, 52

Scaean Gate, 10, 13, 15, 19
Schliemann, Heinrich, 8
Scott, Sir Walter, 48
Scott-Moncrieff, C. K., 25, 28
Seteais, (Portugal), 45, 57, 59
Seville, 78, 95, 116
Shakespeare, William, 16, 116, 128
Sketch Book of Geoffrey Crayon, Gent., The (Irving), 78, 88
Siberia, 62, 67–68, 72
Sicily, 68
Sidon/Sidonian, 13
Sierra Morena (Spain), 125–126
Sierra Nevada (Spain), 87, 91, 95
Sintra, 36, 43–51, 53–60, 77, 86, 103
Slavophile, 62, 74
Sleepy Hollow (Irving), 78
Smerdyakov, Pavel Fyodorovich (Dostoyevsky), 71
Smyrna, 9, 57
South Carolina, 107
Southey, Robert, 53, 55
Spain/Spanish, 37, 54, 77, 79–80, 84–86, 88–89, 91, 95, 108, 115–122, 125–129, 132
Sparta, 10
Statius, Publius Papinius, 22
Stormfield, 111
Strakhov, Nikolay Nikolayevitch, 74
Strata VIIa, 8, 23
Straw Market (Florence), 69
Swann, Charles (Proust), 26, 28, 30, 32–33, 38–39
Swann's way, 30
Swann's Way, 28
Switzerland, 62, 76
Svidrigaylov, Arkady Ivanovich (Dostoyevsky), 75

Tagus River, 44, 46, 52
Tansonville (Proust), 38–39
Tasso, Battista del, 69
Thoreau, Henry David, 106, 133–145, 147–155

Tivoli Sintra, Hotel, 58
Toboso, El (Spain), 118–119, 122–124, 130
Toledo, 115–116
Torcheux, Virginie (Proust), 36
Torres Vedras (Portugal), 49
Tower of Justice (Spain), 91
Tribune, (New York), 97
Troilus, 16–23
Troilus and Cressida (Chaucer), 7, 16, 23
Trojan Horse, 9
Trojan War, 8, 9, 18, 23
Trojans, 8, 10–11, 13–15, 17
Troy, 7–24, 61
Truro, Mass., 136, 141, 143, 148, 151
Turgenev, Ivan Sergeyevich, 75
Turkey/Turkish, 9, 18, 45, 93, 116
Twain, Mark, 73, 93, 97–113, 115, 124
Twain, Mark, Memorial, 110, 112

Uffizi Museum, 67–68, 74
United States, 89

Valdepeñas, 122
Vathek (Beckford), 45, 49, 51
Venice, 74, 98–107, 109–110, 112–113, 124
Vevey (Switzerland), 66
Victoria, Queen, 52
Victorian, 37
Vienna, 74

Vinteuil (Proust), 26
Virgil, 16, 23
Vivonne River, (Proust), 28, 33–39, 40
Voltaire, François Marie, 66
Vox Clamantis (Gower), 17

Walden (Thoreau), 135
Walden Pond, Mass., 134, 136
Washington Irving Hotel (Spain), 90
Wedgwood, 93
Weil, Jeanne (Proust), 36
Wellfleet, Mass., 136–137, 139, 151, 154
West/Westerners, 75–76
Wiesbaden (Germany), 74
Wife of Bath (Chaucer), 80
Williams, Stanley, 83–84, 87, 89
Winter Notes on Summer Impressions (Dostoyevsky), 74
Within a Budding Grove (Proust), 28
World War II, 51

Ximines, Mateo (Irving), 80, 87, 91, 93

Yale University, 83
Yankee, 108, 141
Yarmolinsky, Avrahm, 74

Zeus, 9–10
Zitza (Greece), 46, 51